Love is a canvas furnished by nature and embroidered
by imagination ...
VOLTAIRE

Anne-Katrin Weber

IN LOVE WITH

PARIS

RECIPES & STORIES FROM
THE MOST ROMANTIC CITY
IN THE WORLD

RECIPE PHOTOGRAPHS
Julia Hoersch

MOOD PHOTOGRAPHS
Nathalie Geffroy

Hardie Grant
BOOKS

NOTE: All oven temperatures provided are for non-fan-assisted ovens. If you are using a fan-assisted oven, reduce the temperatures by 20°C/70°F.

THE MOST BEAUTIFUL PARKS

ABOVE THE CITY'S ROOFTOPS

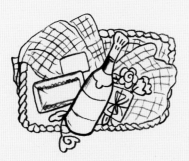

A CULINARY
STROLL THROUGH
THE CITY OF LOVE

Paris! Dreamy alleys, romantic parks and little cafés – and delicious food wherever you go. We will meander through the city, the magic of the French language in our ears, and in our heads all the films, stories, poems, musicals and chansons … We will encounter Abelard and Héloïse, who are forever united in the Père Lachaise cemetery, recall the tragic love of the Hunchback of Notre-Dame, our first kiss in the Parc Monceau and Baudelaire's poem *To a Passer-by*. Love is everywhere here!

Stroll with us as we cross picturesque bridges, traverse old *quartiers*, treat ourselves to a break in the Jardin du Luxembourg and go with the flow like Gil Pender in *Midnight in Paris*. Our hearts will beat faster when the scent of freshly baked croissants wafts through the morning air and tempting tartlets and macarons from the patisseries enhance the afternoon. We will enjoy ourselves picnicking on baguettes and cheese, and with a nice glass of Bordeaux in our hand we will watch the colourful street life or spoil ourselves with a crème brûlée at Les Deux Moulins. And by the evening at the latest, with the day drawing to a close as we marvel at the sparkling Eiffel Tower, we will without a doubt be in love – with Paris!

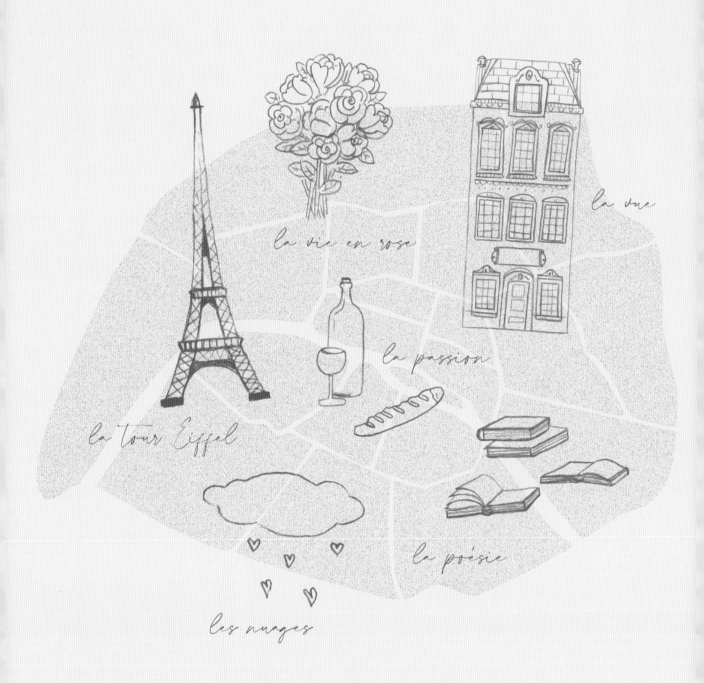

la vie en rose

la vue

la passion

la tour Eiffel

la poésie

les nuages

Paris

ABOVE THE CITY'S ROOFTOPS

Whether in the alleys of Montmartre,
on a little Paris balcony or up in the
illuminated Eiffel Tower — with the city
of love at your feet, your heart beats
that much faster.

A WALK
THROUGH THE *QUARTIER*
OF LOVE

On the city's highest hill is the artists' *quartier* MONTMARTRE. The charming alleys with their cobblestones and steep steps tempt you to saunter, and in the cosy cafés, bistros and bars of this district you can luxuriate in the ambience of Paris.

Probably Montmartre's best-known café is the CAFÉ DES DEUX MOULINS, the workplace of Amélie Poulain in the film *Amélie*. This is where she first meets Nino Quincampoix, a collector of discarded photo booth photos, with whom she has fallen in love.

If you walk from this café in the direction of the SACRÉ-COEUR BASILICA, you will pass the SQUARE JEHAN RICTUS. With its MUR DES JE T'AIME this little garden is the ideal spot to declare your love, as its famous mural bears the words: 'I love you' in over 300 different languages and dialects.

Once you have arrived at the front of the basilica, you can sit down on the steps, listen to the buskers and cast your eye over hidden vineyards, small streets and other romantic locations.

PARIS-BREST

FOR THE CHOUX PASTRY

100 ml (3½ fl oz/scant ½ cup) milk

100 g (3½ oz) butter

2½ tsp sugar

Pinch of salt

150 g (5 oz/1¼ cups) plain (all-purpose) flour

4 eggs (medium)

40 g (1½ oz) flaked (slivered) almonds

FOR THE FILLING

50 g (2 oz) hazelnuts

75 g (2½ oz/⅓ cup) sugar

15 g (½ oz) butter

500 ml (17 fl oz/2 cups) double (heavy) cream

PLUS

1 tbsp icing (confectioner's) sugar

1. To make the choux pastry, bring 150 ml (5 fl oz/scant ⅔ cup) of water and the milk, butter, sugar and salt to the boil in a saucepan. Remove from the heat, add the flour and stir vigorously with a wooden spoon, then return the pan to the heat. Stir the mixture over a medium heat until it is smooth and forms a white coating on the bottom of the pan. Transfer to a bowl and thoroughly mix in one of the eggs. Using a hand-held mixer with a dough hook attachment, add the remaining eggs one at a time, stirring well until you have a smooth dough. Add the dough to a piping bag with a large star-shaped nozzle.

2. Preheat the oven to 190°C (375°F/gas 5). Line two baking sheets with baking parchment. Squeeze the pastry dough out onto the sheets to form about 10 rings (9 cm/3½ in in diameter), leaving a little space between them, as the dough will rise slightly. Sprinkle the dough rings with the flaked almonds. Bake in the oven for 20–25 minutes until golden brown, but do not open the oven during the first 15 minutes or the pastry will collapse. Remove from the oven, cut through horizontally and leave to cool.

3. To make the filling, finely chop the hazelnuts. Over a low heat slowly melt the sugar in a saucepan to form a pale-coloured caramel. Stir in the butter and hazelnuts until the nuts are coated with caramel, then quickly spread the mixture onto a sheet of baking parchment. Leave to cool and go hard, then chop to form a fine brittle in a food processor. Beat the cream until stiff. Fold in the brittle, add the mixture to a piping bag with a large, flat nozzle and squeeze onto the lower choux-pastry ring. Cover with the top ring and sprinkle with icing sugar.

PREPARATION TIME: about 1 hour
BAKING TIME: 20–25 minutes
MAKES 10

SALADE NIÇOISE

FOR THE SALAD

4 eggs (medium)

150 g (5 oz) fine green beans

½ lettuce (e.g. romaine or Batavia)

100 g (3½ oz) cherry tomatoes

1 gherkin

1 white onion

3–4 sprigs of basil

50 g (2 oz) pitted black olives

4–8 anchovy fillets (marinated in oil)

2 tuna steaks (each approx. 200 g / 7 oz)

2 tbsp olive oil

FOR THE VINAIGRETTE

1–2 garlic cloves

3 tbsp red wine vinegar

1 tsp Dijon mustard

8 tbsp very good olive oil

salt and freshly ground black pepper

1. Hard-boil the eggs for 10 minutes, rinse in cold water, peel and halve. Wash the beans, boil in salted water for 8–10 minutes until al dente, then pour off the water, rinse in cold water and drain. Clean the lettuce and pull the leaves into smaller pieces. Halve the cherry tomatoes. Cut the gherkin into thin slices. Peel the onion and cut into fine rings. Rinse the basil, pat dry and tear into small pieces.

2. For the vinaigrette, peel the garlic. Stir in the vinegar, mustard, a generous pinch of salt and plenty of pepper, then crush the garlic and add. Drizzle in the oil and stir to make a creamy sauce.

3. Arrange the lettuce leaves with the eggs, beans, tomatoes, gherkin, onion, olives and anchovies on a wide platter. Drizzle the vinaigrette over the salad and sprinkle the basil on top.

4. Rinse the tuna in cold water and pat dry. Heat the oil in a frying pan (skillet) and sear the tuna steaks for about 1 minute on each side, so it is well browned on the outside but still raw to translucent on the inside. Fry for 1–2 minutes longer if you prefer your tuna well done. Season with salt and pepper, and remove from the heat. Halve the tuna steaks and serve on top of the salad.

PREPARATION TIME: about 45 minutes

SERVES 4

GREEN
PEA SOUP

1 onion

1–2 garlic cloves

300 g (10½ oz) potatoes (floury)

2 tbsp butter

100 ml (3½ fl oz/scant ½ cup) white wine

1 bay leaf

2 sprigs of thyme

approx. 1.2 litres (40 fl oz/4¾ cups) vegetable or chicken stock

450 g (1 lb) peas (frozen)

freshly grated nutmeg

salt and freshly ground black pepper

PLUS

2 slices of white bread or toast

2 tbsp butter

handful of pea sprouts

2–3 sprigs of purple basil

100 g (3½ fl oz/½ cup) crème fraîche

1. Peel and finely dice the onion and garlic. Peel the potatoes and cut into small cubes. Foam the butter in a saucepan and sweat the diced onion in it until it becomes transparent. Add the garlic and cook with the onion for a short while. Pour in the white wine and briefly reduce. Add the potatoes, bay leaf, thyme and vegetable stock. Bring back to the boil, and then boil for 10–15 minutes with the lid on, until the potatoes are soft.

2. Remove the bay leaf and thyme. Add the peas. Bring the soup to the boil again, finely purée in a food blender or using a hand-held blender and season with the nutmeg and salt and pepper to taste.

3. To make the croûtons, cut the bread into small cubes. Foam the butter in a saucepan and fry the diced bread until the cubes are crispy all over. Season to taste with salt and pepper and drain the excess fat off on some paper towel. Rinse the pea sprouts and basil, and pat dry. Tear the basil leaves into smaller pieces.

4. To serve, heat the soup and pour into soup bowls. Stir in a little crème fraîche and decorate with croûtons, pea sprouts and basil.

PREPARATION TIME: about 35 minutes
SERVES 4

19

KING PRAWNS
WITH PASTIS AND TOMATOES

750 g (1 lb 1 oz) king prawns
with heads and shells (approx. 24)

200 g (7 oz) cherry tomatoes

2 shallots

2 garlic cloves

1 organic lemon

2 sprigs of basil

6 tbsp olive oil

3 tbsp pastis

1 tbsp butter

sea salt

smoked paprika

1. Rinse the prawns in cold water, pat dry, fully peel and de-vein. Halve the tomatoes. Peel the shallots and garlic, and cut into thin slices. Rinse the lemon in hot water, pat dry and cut into slices. Rinse the basil, pat dry, pluck off the leaves and chop coarsely.

2. Heat the olive oil in a very large pan (or two pans), then briefly sweat the shallots and garlic. Increase the temperature, add the prawns and sliced lemon, and sauté all over for 2–3 minutes over a high heat. Deglaze with the pastis, add the tomatoes and butter, and continue to fry over a high heat for 2–3 minutes, tossing occasionally. Season to taste with sea salt and paprika, mix in the basil and serve immediately.

PREPARATION TIME: about 25 minutes
SERVES 4

POULET RÔTI

1 corn-fed poularde or 1 large free-range
chicken (approx. 1.5 kg/3lb 5 oz)

5 garlic cloves

6 bay leaves

2 sprigs of rosemary

1 organic lemon

*freshly ground **black pepper***

*50 g (2 oz) very soft **butter***

*250 ml (8½ fl oz/1 cup) **chicken stock***

salt and freshly ground
black pepper

1. Preheat the oven to 200°C (400°C/gas 6). Rinse the inside and outside of the chicken in cold water, and pat dry. Squeeze the cloves of garlic and stuff the chicken with half of the garlic together with the bay leaves and rosemary. Wash the lemon in hot water, pat dry and cut into slices.

2. Truss the chicken, season to taste with salt and pepper, brush all over with the butter, then lay it breast side down in an ovenproof dish. Pour over the chicken stock and add the remaining cloves of garlic and sliced lemon. Loosely cover the dish with a sheet of aluminium foil. Roast in the oven for 30 minutes, occasionally basting with the stock.

3. Turn the chicken so it is breast side up, and cook uncovered (without aluminium foil) for a further 40 minutes, until crispy and nicely browned. Cover and rest for 5 minutes before serving.

PREPARATION TIME: about 20 minutes
COOKING TIME: about 1 hour 10 minutes
SERVES 4

⌒♡⌒

ŒUFS EN COCOTTE

1 tbsp soft butter

4 large white mushrooms

40 g (1½ oz) gruyère

1 tbsp parsley leaves

150 g (5 oz/⅔ cup) crème fraîche

freshly ground black pepper

4 eggs (medium)

4–8 slices of baguette

*salt and freshly ground
black pepper*

26

1. Preheat the oven to 180°C (350°F/gas 4). Generously grease four ramekins with the soft butter. Clean the mushrooms, wipe with a dish towel and cut into thin slices. Finely grate the cheese. Finely chop the parsley and stir in the crème fraîche and a little salt and pepper.

2. Spoon half the herby crème fraîche into the ramekins. Add the mushrooms and cheese. Break an egg into each of the ramekins. Put the remaining herby crème fraîche on top.

3. Place the ramekins in a wide gratin dish and pour in plenty of hot water, so the ramekins are two-thirds immersed. Put the dish on the middle shelf of the oven and bake the eggs for 15–20 minutes; the whites should be firm, but the yolks still soft.

4. Shortly before serving, toast the baguette. To eat, dip the baguette into the eggs.

PREPARATION TIME: about 15 minutes
COOKING TIME: 15–20 minutes
SERVES 4

CÔTE DE BŒUF
WITH SAUCE BÉARNAISE

FOR THE MEAT

approx. 1.2 kg (2 lb 11 oz) **rib of beef** *(côte de bœuf)*

2 tbsp **olive oil**

sea salt *and freshly ground* **black pepper**

2–3 small sprigs of **rosemary**

FOR THE SAUCE BÉARNAISE

1 **shallot**

2 sprigs of **tarragon**

100 ml (3½ fl oz/scant ½ cup) **dry white wine**

3 tbsp **white wine vinegar**

5 **peppercorns**

200 g (7 oz) **butter**

3 very fresh **egg yolks**

1–2 pinches of **sugar**

1–2 squeezes of fresh **lemon juice**

1. Take the beef out of the fridge at least 1 hour before roasting. Slightly cut the beef away from the bone (but not completely) and preheat the oven to 160°C (320°F/gas 2). Heat the oil in a cast-iron pan or roasting pan. Season the beef well with salt and pepper, sear for about 5 minutes on each side over a medium to high heat and cook in the oven for 20–25 minutes Then open the oven door and rest the beef in the oven for 5 minutes.

2. Meanwhile, to make the sauce béarnaise, peel and finely dice the shallot. Rinse the tarragon, pat dry and chop the leaves very finely. Bring the shallot along with the white wine, white wine vinegar and peppercorns to the boil in a small saucepan and reduce by half. Coarsely dice the butter and melt in a second saucepan, then bring to the boil and continue to boil over a low heat for 5–10 minutes, until the white whey clearly separates off and the butter clarifies. Ladle the whey off with a spoon.

3. Pour water into a small saucepan to a depth of 2–3 cm (¾–¼ in) and bring to the boil. Pour the egg yolks into a stainless-steel mixing bowl, then sieve the white-wine mixture onto them, thoroughly squeezing out the diced shallot. Place the bowl on a bain-marie (not allowing the bowl to come into contact with the water, otherwise the egg yolks may curdle). Beat the egg-yolk mixture with a whisk or a hand-held mixer with a beater attachment for 2–3 minutes until it is thick, foamy and pale in colour.

4. Beat the warm butter into the egg foam, initially drop by drop, then in a thin stream. Stir in the tarragon. Season the sauce to taste with the salt, sugar and lemon juice. Cut the beef into slices and serve with the sauce.

PREPARATION TIME: about 45 minutes
SERVES 4

29

FORBIDDEN LOVE

The **PÈRE LACHAISE** cemetery is tempting to visit not only because of the views it affords of the city but also because of the opportunity it offers to admire the graves of great artists, authors and musicians. As well as Oscar Wilde, Jim Morrison and Frédéric Chopin, here lie two people whose tragic love story made them one of the most famous pairs of lovers of the Middle Ages – Héloïse and Abelard.

In early 12th-century Paris, the young Héloïse and her much older tutor Peter Abelard fell in love. They kept their love a secret until Héloïse became pregnant. In fear of her Uncle Fulbert, Héloïse fled with Abelard to live with his family, where they brought their son Astrolabe into the world.

In the meantime, Abelard sought reconciliation with Fulbert by offering to marry Héloïse and thus restore her honour – though the marriage was to remain secret, so as not to damage his reputation and career. Fulbert agreed, and the couple wed.

But when Fulbert made the couple's marriage known, Abelard took his wife to a convent for protection. Fulbert saw this as a cowardly act on the part of Abelard, perpetrated in order to shirk his marital duties, and had him castrated. Deeply aggrieved, Abelard retreated to a monastery.

Abelard and Héloïse, who became a respected abbess, never saw each other again, but to the end of their days they wrote each other love letters, which are still deeply moving to read.

CRÈME BRÛLÉE

1 vanilla pod (bean)

400 ml (13 fl oz/generous 1½ cups) **double**
(heavy) cream

5 cm (2 in) piece of **organic orange peel**

5 **egg yolks** *(medium)*

5 tbsp **sugar**

2 tsp **orange-blossom water** *(optional)*

1. Slit open the vanilla pod lengthways and scrape out the seeds. Bring the cream, orange peel, vanilla pod and seeds to the boil in a saucepan, remove from the heat and let the vanilla cream steep for 10 minutes. Beat the egg yolks and 2 tablespoons of sugar together until fluffy, sieve the vanilla cream, then stir in with orange-blossom water (if using). Pour the mixture into four ovenproof ramekins or wide cups.

2. Preheat the oven to 120°C (250°F/gas ½). Place the ramekins or wide cups in a large gratin dish and pour hot water into the dish until the ramekins are two-thirds immersed. Place the dish on the middle shelf of the oven and cook for 45 minutes. Remove the ramekins from the water, allow the cream mixture to cool, cover and refrigerate for 4 hours.

3. To caramelise the tops of the crème brûlées, put the ramekins back in the gratin dish and pour iced water around them to keep the cream mixture nice and cold while it caramelises. Sprinkle the ramekins evenly with the remaining sugar and briefly caramelise with a blowtorch. Serve immediately.

PREPARATION TIME: about 25 minutes
COOKING TIME: 45 minutes · **COOLING TIME**: 4 hours
SERVES 4

33

CHEESE SOUFFLÉ

50 g (2 oz) *butter*

30 g (1 oz/¼ cup) *plain*
(all-purpose) flour

250 ml (8½ fl oz/1 cup)
full-fat milk

5 *eggs* (medium)

125 g (4 oz) *blue cheese*
(e.g. Bleu d'Auvergne)

freshly grated *nutmeg*

salt and freshly ground
black pepper

1. Melt the butter in a saucepan and leave to cool until luke warm. Grease the soufflé dish with 1 teaspoon of the lukewarm butter. Fold one sheet of baking parchment lengthways and line the dish so the parchment projects about 3 cm (1¼ in)over the sides. Also brush the baking parchment with 1–2 teaspoons of liquid butter.

2. Reheat the remaining butter, sprinkle in the flour and stir well to create a roux. Remove the saucepan from the heat, gradually add the milk and stir thoroughly to stop lumps forming. Return the saucepan to the heat, then heat the sauce and boil for 3 minutes, stirring constantly. Remove the saucepan from the heat.

3. Separate the eggs. Finely crush the cheese with the back of a fork and mix into the warm sauce until it has melted. Stir in four of the egg yolks, one at a time. Generously season the mixture to taste with salt, pepper and nutmeg, and pour into a bowl.

4. Preheat the oven to 200°C (400°C/gas 6). Beat all five egg whites with a pinch of salt until very stiff. Stir a quarter of the whipped egg whites into the cheese mixture, then carefully but thoroughly fold in the remainder. Pour the mixture into the dish and bake the soufflé for 20–25 minutes, until it has risen well and browned nicely. To check whether the soufflé is cooked, insert a metal skewer. When you pull the skewer out, if it is almost dry or only slightly moist, then the soufflé is ready. Serve immediately, so the soufflé doesn't collapse.

PREPARATION TIME: about 30 minutes
BAKING TIME: 20–25 minutes
SERVES 4

ARTICHOKES
WITH SAUCE GRIBICHE

FOR THE ARTICHOKES

4 large artichokes

3 tbsp lemon juice

salt

FOR THE SAUCE GRIBICHE

2 eggs (medium)

1 tbsp capers (from a jar)

4 gherkins (from a jar)

2–3 sprigs each of tarragon and chives

200 g (7 oz / ¾ cup) mayonnaise

50 g (2 oz / ¼ cup) yoghurt

1 heaped tsp whole-grain mustard

Pinch of sugar

salt and freshly ground black pepper

1. For the artichokes, bring plenty of water to the boil in a large saucepan together with a little salt and the lemon juice. Break off the artichoke stems so the hard fibres are pulled out of the base, and cut off the stem bases to flatten them. Remove the outer petals of the artichokes and cut off about a third of the remaining petals with a sharp serrated knife. Put the artichokes in the boiling water and simmer for 30–40 minutes. The artichokes will be cooked when the lower petals can be pulled off easily.

2. Meanwhile, to make the sauce gribiche, hard-boil the eggs for about 10 minutes, rinse in cold water, peel and finely chop. Drain and finely chop the capers and gherkins. Rinse the tarragon and chive sprigs, and pat dry. Pluck off the tarragon leaves and finely chop, then cut the chives into small rings. Mix everything in a bowl, then stir in the mayonnaise, yoghurt and mustard, and season with 1–2 tablespoons of the liquid from the gherkins, the sugar and salt and pepper to taste.

3. Remove the artichokes from the water with a slotted spoon, turn them upside down and briefly drain. Then serve with the sauce gribiche. To eat, pull the petals off one by one and dip them in the sauce. Once all the fleshy petals have been plucked off, detach the tender purple petals, remove the fuzzy choke, thereby exposing the artichoke heart, and enjoy together with the remaining sauce.

PREPARATION TIME: 10 minutes
COOKING TIME: 30–40 minutes
SERVES 4

TO ABELARD

(extract)

The pleasures of lovers which we share have been too sweet – they can never displease me, and can scarcely be banished from my thoughts.

Wherever I turn they are always there before my eyes, bringing with them awakened longings and fantasies which will not let me sleep.

Even during the celebration of Mass, when our prayers should be purer, lewd visions of those pleasures take such a hold upon my unhappy soul that my thoughts are on their wantonness instead of on my prayers. I should be groaning over the sins I have committed, but I can only sigh for what I have lost.

39

MOULES MARINIÈRES

1 onion

2 garlic cloves

1 small celery stalk

1 carrot

1 thin leek

2.5 kg (5 lb 10 oz) mussels

3 tbsp olive oil

300 ml (10 fl oz / 1¼ cup) white wine

4 sprigs of thyme

2 bay leaves

½ bunch of parsley

salt and freshly ground black pepper

40

1. Peel and finely dice the onion and garlic. Clean the celery, carrot and leek, then finely dice the celery and carrot and cut the leek into thin rings. Put the mussels in a large sieve, wash thoroughly under cold running water, remove the beards and discard any open mussels.

2. Heat the olive oil in a large, wide saucepan. Sweat the vegetables for about 3 minutes. Pour in the white wine, add the thyme and bay leaves, then season to taste with salt and pepper and heat. Add the mussels, then put the lid on the saucepan and steam over a medium heat for about 7 minutes, carefully stirring them a little now and then.

3. Meanwhile, rinse the parsley, pat dry, pluck off the leaves and chop coarsely. Remove the lid from the saucepan and discard any mussels that are still closed. Plate up the mussels and the broth in bowls, and sprinkle with parsley. Serve with French fries or baguettes.

PREPARATION TIME: about 30 minutes
SERVES 4

41

TARTE TATIN

*approx. 1.5 kg (3 lb 5 oz) **tart apples***
(e.g. Cox's Orange Pippin or Braeburn)

*150 g (5 oz / ⅔ cup) **sugar***

*100 g (3½ oz) **butter***

2 packs (each 280 g / 10 oz)
***puff-pastry rounds** (refrigerated)*

*250 g (9 oz / 1 cup) **crème fraîche***

*3 tbsp **Calvados** (apple brandy)*

*1 tbsp mild **honey***

1. Peel and quarter the apples and remove the cores. Slowly melt the sugar in a tarte tatin or flameproof/ovenproof dish 26 cm (10 in) in diameter over a low heat until it caramelises and turns a pale brown colour. Stir in the butter in small flakes, then remove the dish from the heat. Arrange the apple quarters upright and close together in the still-soft caramel. Return the dish to the heat and simmer the apples in the caramel for 10 minutes. This will evaporate some of the liquid and slightly caramelise the apples.

2. Meanwhile, take the puff pastry out of the fridge and bring to room temperature for 5 minutes. Preheat the oven to 200°C (400°F/gas 6). Lay the two pastry rounds on top of each other over the apples, tucking the pastry edges between the edge of the dish and the apples. Prick the pastry several times with a fork. Bake for 30–35 minutes, or until the pastry is light brown and crispy.

3. Stir the crème fraîche, Calvados and honey together in a bowl. Remove the dish from the oven, lay an inverted cake plate on top of the tarte and turn it out onto the plate. Take care, as some of the hot juice may trickle out. Cut the tarte into slices and serve with the Calvados cream.

PREPARATION TIME: 30 minutes
BAKING TIME: 30–35 minutes
SERVES 8-10

43

ROMANTIC OUTINGS À DEUX

If you wish to spend the tail end of the day above the rooftops of **MONTMARTRE**, you should make your way to the city's highest park – **PARC DES BUTTES-CHAUMONT**. Yews, pines, cedars and pagoda trees grace this magical place, and there's a lake with an island, a waterfall and a grotto. Why not take a decent bottle of wine with you and enjoy the sunset on one of the park's many meadows!

If you're seeking a little more privacy, try the neighbouring **BUTTE BERGEYRE**. This park overlooking a small vineyard is a secluded spot for lovers, and offers a fabulous view of the **SACRÉ CŒUR**.

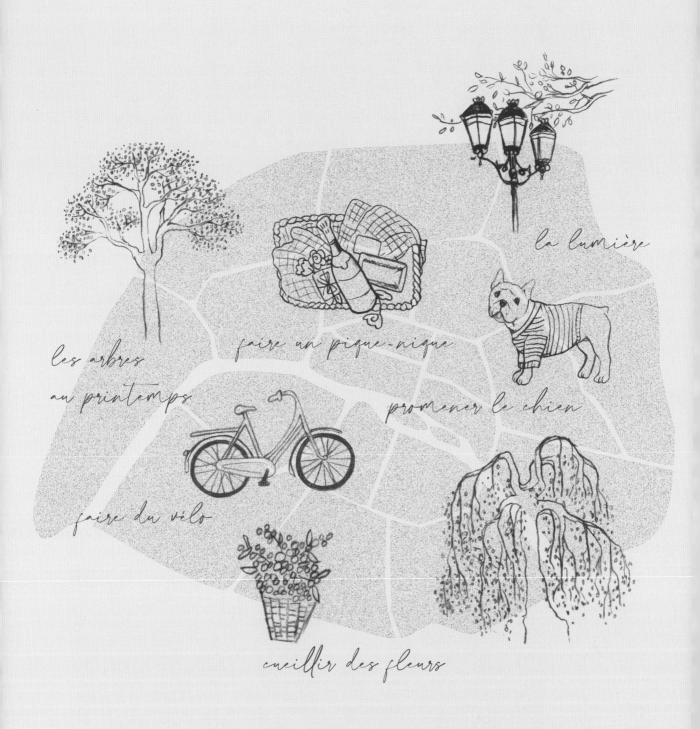

la lumière

les arbres
au printemps

faire un pique-nique

promener le chien

faire du vélo

cueillir des fleurs

Paris

THE MOST BEAUTIFUL PARKS

Paris boasts a wealth of green oases for
lingering and sauntering, and where couples
can spend time together on a relaxed walk
or enjoy a real French picnic *à deux*.

TOMATO TARTLETS

FOR THE SHORTCRUST PASTRY

250 g (9 oz/2 cups) **plain (all-purpose) flour**

½ tsp **salt**

120 g (4 oz) **cold butter**

30 g (1 oz) finely grated **Parmesan**

1 egg (medium)

FOR THE HERB OIL

1 bunch each of **basil** *and* **parsley**

150 ml (5 fl oz/⅔ cup) **good olive oil**

FOR THE TOPPING

150 g (5 oz) **soft goat's milk cheese**

100 g (3½ oz/½ cup) **crème fraîche**

250 g (9 oz) mixed-colour **cherry tomatoes**

salt and freshly ground **black pepper**

1 tbsp **basil leaves**

PLUS

dried pulses

1. Mix the flour and salt on a work surface. Cut the cold butter into small flakes and rub into the flour with your fingers until you have a fine crumb. Add the Parmesan, egg and 2–3 tablespoons of cold water, and knead everything to form a smooth ball of pastry dough. Wrap the dough in cling film (plastic wrap) and rest in the fridge for 30 minutes.

2. To make the herb oil, rinse the herbs, pat dry, pluck off the leaves and whizz with the olive oil in a food blender or processor until smooth.

3. Preheat the oven to 200°C (400°F/gas 6) and grease 6 tartlet tins. Dust the work surface with a little flour, roll out the pastry dough and cut out six pastry bases using 12 cm (5 in) cookie cutters. Line the greased tins with the circles of pastry, then prick the pastry bases several times with a fork. Cover with baking parchment and add a few dried pulses to each tartlet (to bake-blind). Bake at the bottom of the oven for 20–25 minutes, until the pastry bases are golden brown and crispy. Take out of the oven and remove the baking parchment and pulses. Briefly cool the tartlets, then remove from the tins and allow to cool fully on a cooling rack.

4. Shortly before serving, stir the goat's milk cheese and crème fraîche together in a bowl until creamy, and season to taste with salt and pepper. Cut the tomatoes into thin slices. Spread the creamed cheese onto the tartlets, arrange the tomato slices on top and garnish with basil. Drizzle with herb oil and serve.

PREPARATION TIME: about 40 minutes plus resting time
BAKING TIME: 20–25 minutes
SERVES 6

RED-WINE PEARS

125 g (4 oz / ½ cup) **sugar**

600 ml (20 fl oz / 2½ cup) strong **red wine**

1 **cinnamon stick**

3 **cloves**

1 **bay leaf**

5 cm (2 in) piece of **organic orange peel**

4 firm but ripe medium-sized **pears**

2 tsp **cornflour (cornstarch)**

1. Melt the sugar in a saucepan over a low heat. Pour in the red wine, add the stick of cinnamon, cloves, bay leaf and orange peel and boil the liquid for about 2 minutes until the sugar has dissolved.

2. Meanwhile, peel the pears, but leave in the stalks. Stand the pears upright in the spiced red wine, put the lid on the saucepan and gently simmer for 15–25 minutes. The cooking time largely depends on the type of pears used and their ripeness, so now and again insert a small kitchen knife, to check whether they are done. Lift the cooked pears out of the poaching liquid with a slotted spoon.

3. Stir the cornflour into 2 tablespoons of cold water until smooth. Bring the poaching liquid to the boil and blend with the cornflour. Remove the pan from the heat, then put the pears in the syrup while it cools, allowing them to steep.

PREPARATION TIME: about 30 minutes plus cooling time
SERVES 4

ALWAYS
IN QUEST OF LOVE

One of world literature's most famous and most beautiful love stories starts in the **JARDIN DU LUXEMBOURG**. In Victor Hugo's novel *Les Misérables*, one beautiful spring day in the early 19th century the young Cosette and the student Marius fall in love in this park. For those of you who haven't read the book, the couple's story doesn't end half as badly as the title might suggest.

The gardens are to be found between the lively **SAINT-GERMAIN-DES-PRÉS** *quartier* and the **QUARTIER LATIN**, which Parisians also lovingly call 'Le Luco'. They were commissioned by Maria de' Medici following the death of her husband King Henry IV of France, and were inspired by the Boboli Gardens in her home city of Florence. As well as being a wonderful place, the Jardin du Luxembourg also accommodates an apple orchard, greenhouses full of roses and orchids, an orangery and an apiary – the perfect place for a break on one of the pretty park benches.

CHOCOLATE
MACARONS

FOR THE MERINGUE SHELLS

80 g (3 oz/¾ cup) **ground blanched lmonds (almond meal)**

135 g (5 oz/1 cup) **icing (confectioner's) sugar**

4 tsp **cocoa (unsweetened chocolate) powder**

60 g (2 oz) **egg white** *(1–2 days old)*

Pinch of **salt**

Squeeze of fresh **lemon juice**

1 tsp **sugar**

FOR THE FILLING

75 g (2½ oz) **dark chocolate** *(at least 70 per cent cocoa solids)*

5 tbsp **double (heavy) cream**

20 g (¾ oz) **butter**

1. To make the meringue shells, mix the almonds, icing sugar and cocoa in a bowl, then grind very finely in batches in a food processor or blender. Pass this mixture through a fine-meshed sieve. Beat the egg white with the salt and lemon juice until stiff. Slowly add the sugar, and continue to beat the egg white until it is firm enough to cut. Stir the almond mixture into the beaten egg white in three portions, pressing some of the air out owith the back of the spoon as you do so. This should create a thick, homogeneous batter.

2. Add the mixture to a piping bag with a medium-sized nozzle. Pipe 40 equal-sized dollops (about 3 cm/1¼ in in diameter) onto a baking sheet lined with baking parchment, leaving spaces between them. Once all the macarons have been piped out, tap the bottom of the baking sheet with your hand a few times. Leave to dry for 20–30 minutes at room temperature.

3. Preheat the oven to 140°C (280°F/gas 3). Bake the macarons for 14 minutes. Carefully remove the baking parchment together with the macarons from the baking sheet and allow to cool, and only then remove them from the parchment.

4. To make the filling, break the chocolate into pieces, and heat with the cream in a small saucepan over a medium heat until it has melted. Whisk the butter in well. The chocolate butter cream should now be spreadable – otherwise put it in the fridge for a short while. Add the cream to a piping bag with a small nozzle and pipe onto half of the meringue shells. Top with the remaining shells.

PREPARATION TIME: about 1 hour
BAKING TIME: about 15 minutes
MAKES 20

57

VICTOR HUGO

LES MISÉRABLES

(extract)

One day the air was warm, the Luxembourg was inundated with
light and shade, the sky was as pure as though angels had
washed it that morning, the sparrows were giving vent to
little twitters in the depths of the chestnut trees

Marius had thrown open his whole soul to nature, he was not thinking of anything, he simply lived and breathed, he passed near the bench, the young girl raised her eyes to him, the two glances met.

What was there in the young girl's glance on this occasion? Marius could not have told. There was nothing and there was everything. It was a strange flash.

She dropped her eyes, and he pursued his way. What he had just seen was no longer the ingenuous and simple eye of a child; it was a mysterious gulf which had half opened, then abruptly closed again.

There comes a day when the young girl glances in this manner. Woe to him who chances to be there!

That first gaze of a soul which does not, as yet, know itself, is like the dawn in the sky. It is the awakening of something radiant and strange. Nothing can give any idea of the dangerous charm of that unexpected gleam, which flashes suddenly and vaguely forth from adorable shadows, and which is composed of all the innocence of the present, and of all the passion of the future. It is a sort of undecided tenderness which reveals itself by chance, and which waits. It is a snare which the innocent maiden sets unknown to herself, and in which she captures hearts without either wishing or knowing it.

59

IN THE FOOTSTEPS OF
MARIE ANTOINETTE

The **PARC DE BAGATELLE** in the west of the city is a wonderful place of calm, and its history is at least as beautiful as the gardens themselves.

Legend has it that the park was a token of the Comte d'Artois' love for his sister-in-law Marie Antoinette. In the summer of 1777, before embarking on a two-month journey, the young queen had bet him that by her return he would not manage to transform his dilapidated pavilion in the **BOIS DE BOULOGNE** into a luxurious château with grounds and give her a worthy reception. The ambitious count commissioned an architect, who drew up the plans for the project overnight. More than 900 craftsmen worked night and day on getting the château and gardens ready in time.

The park, with its impressive rose garden, is now ideal for an extended afternoon walk, during which – in memory of Marie Antoinette – a delicious slice of cake is absolutely indispensable.

TARTES FLAMBÉE

FOR THE PASTRY

300 g (10½ oz/2½ cups) plain (all-purpose) flour

salt

FOR THE TOPPING

200 g (7 oz) onions

2 tbsp olive oil

150 g (5 oz) smoked bacon

4 small potatoes

400 g (14 oz/1¾ cup) crème fraîche

1 tbsp thyme leaves

freshly ground black pepper

1. To make the pastry dough, mix the flour, 200 ml (7 fl oz/scant 1 cup) of cold water and 1½ teaspoons of salt in a bowl using a hand-held mixer with a dough hook attachment. Shape the dough into a ball, cover and leave to rest for a few minutes.

2. Meanwhile, to make the topping, peel the onions, halve them and cut into fine strips. Heat the oil in a saucepan, and over a medium heat sweat the onions for 5–10 minutes until light yellow. Remove the pan from the heat. Cut the bacon into thin, 5 mm (⅛ in) strips. Peel the potatoes and shave or cut them into very thin slices.

3. Preheat the oven to 230°C (450°F/gas 8) and line two baking sheets with baking parchment. Briefly knead the dough on a lightly floured work surface, divide it in half and roll out each portion on a little flour to form ovals, 3 mm (⅛ in) thick. Lay the ovals on the baking sheets.

4. Spread crème fraîche over the pastry and top with the potatoes, onions and bacon. Season the tarts with pepper and sprinkle with thyme. Either bake one tart at a time or if you are using a fan-assisted oven, put both tarts in the oven at the same time and maybe switch them over after 5 minutes. Bake the tartes for 10–15 minutes until crispy and golden brown, then serve straight from the oven.

PREPARATION TIME: about 30 minutes.
BAKING TIME: 10–15 minutes
SERVES 4

DUCK-BREAST FILLETS WITH CELERIAC PURÉE

FOR THE CELERIAC PURÉE

1 kg (2 lb 4 oz) **celeriac**
(celery root)

100 ml (3½ fl oz/scant ½ cup)
cream

1 tbsp **butter**

freshly grated **nutmeg**

salt and freshly ground
black pepper

FOR THE MEAT AND THE SAUCE

2 **shallots**

2 tsp **rosemary leaves**

4 **juniper berries**

4 small **duck-breast fillets**

1 tbsp **olive oil**

1 tbsp **sugar**

200 ml (7 fl oz/scant 1 cup)
dry red wine

200 ml (7 fl oz/scant 1 cup)
chicken stock

5 tbsp **crème de cassis**

250 g (9 oz) fresh **raspberries**

1. To make the celeriac purée, peel the celeriac and cut into small cubes. Put the diced celeriac in a saucepan, add water to cover and lightly salt. Bring to the boil and continue to boil for about 15 minutes, until the celeriac is soft. Pour off the water and finely purée the celeriac in a food processor or blender with the cream and butter. Season to taste with salt, pepper and nutmeg, cover and keep warm.

2. Preheat the oven to 160°C (320°F/gas 2). To make the sauce, peel and finely dice the shallots, finely chop the rosemary and squeeze the juniper berries. Rinse the duck-breast fillets in cold water and pat dry. Score the skin with a lozenge pattern, though without cutting into the meat. Season the duck to taste with salt and pepper. Heat the oil in a frying pan (skillet), and brown the duck breast, skin side down, over a medium heat for 3–4 minutes, then turn and brown the other side for 2–3 minutes. Remove the duck and place in an ovenproof dish. Finish cooking in the oven for 10 minutes.

3. Pour the frying fat out of the pan, leaving just 2 tablespoons worth. Heat the remaining fat in the pan and sweat the diced shallots until golden yellow. Stir in the sugar. Deglaze with the red wine. Pour in the chicken stock and crème de cassis, and add the rosemary and juniper berries. Bring the sauce to the boil, and continue to boil for 5–10 minutes over a high heat. Remove the juniper berries, add the raspberries, bring the sauce back to the boil and season to taste with salt and pepper.

4. Heat the celeriac purée, while stirring. Remove the duck-breast fillets from the oven, cover and briefly rest, then slice and serve with the celeriac purée and sauce.

PREPARATION TIME: about 40 minutes
SERVES 4

CROISSANTS

500 g (1 lb 2 oz /4 cups) *plain*
(all-purpose) *flour*

25 g (1 oz) *fresh yeast*

50 g (2 oz /¼ cup) *sugar*

1 egg *(medium)*

1¾ tsp *salt*

250 g (9 oz) *butter*

1 egg yolk

1. Add the flour to a bowl. Dissolve the yeast in 250 ml (8½ fl oz/1 cup) of cold water. Add the yeast water, sugar, egg and salt to the flour. Knead in a food processor for 5 minutes to form an elastic dough. Dust the work surface with a little flour, shape the dough into a smooth ball and return to the bowl. Cover with cling film (plastic wrap) and refrigerate for 30 minutes. Roll out the butter between two sheets of baking parchment to form a 20 x 20 cm (8 x 8 in) square, and refrigerate.

2. Take the yeast dough and the sheet of butter out of the fridge. Roll out the dough on a little flour until it is twice as long as the sheet of butter (i.e. creating a rectangle a good 20 x 40 cm/8 x 16 in in size), thoroughly brush off any excess flour with a pastry brush and lay the sheet of butter over one end of it. Fold the other half of the dough over the sheet of butter, then press the dough edges down well.

3. Roll out the dough on the floured work surface until you have doubled its length. Thoroughly brush off any excess flour. For the first folding, fold a third of the dough over to the middle, then fold the other third over it, as when folding a letter. Wrap the dough in foil and refrigerate for 30 minutes. Repeat this rolling-and-folding process three more times, each time turning the sheet of dough through 90 degrees and always thoroughly brushing off the flour.

4. After the fourth rolling-and-folding, roll the dough out to form a rectangle about 50 cm (20 in) long, and with a large knife cut into about 15 long triangles. Cut about 2 cm (¾ in) into the middle of the short side of each triangle, and roll up the triangles starting from the short side, slightly pulling apart the two flaps formed by the cut as you do so. Bend the dough ends to form the typical croissant shape. Lay them tip-down on two baking sheets lined with baking parchment, and cover with the cut-open freezer bag. Leave for 30—45 minutes at room temperature until they have risen slightly.

5. Preheat the oven to 200°C (400°f/gas 6). Whisk the egg yolks and 1 tablespoon of water, and brush the croissants with it. Bake for 20–25 minutes until golden brown (one baking sheet at a time). Remove from the oven and cool.

PREPARATION TIME: about 1 hour 15 minutes · BAKING TIME: 20–25 minutes
COOLING TIME: 2 hours · RISING TIME: 30–45 minutes
MAKES ABOUT 15

GOUGÈRES

60 g (2 oz) *gruyère*

¼ tsp *salt*

pinch of *sugar*

pinch of freshly grated *nutmeg*

40 g (1½ oz) *butter*

60 g (2 oz/½ cup) *plain (all-purpose) flour*

2 *eggs* (medium)

2 tsp each of *poppy seeds* and *sesame seeds*

freshly ground *black pepper*

1. Finely grate the cheese. Bring to the boil 100 ml (3½ fl oz/scant ½ cup) of water, the salt, sugar and nutmeg, a little pepper and the butter, diced, in a small saucepan. Add the flour all at once, and stir in with a wooden spoon. Stir vigorously for 1 minute over a medium heat, until a white layer forms on the bottom of the saucepan. Pour the mixture into a mixing bowl and cool for about 5 minutes.

2. Preheat the oven to 240°C (465°F/gas 9). Stir the eggs into the cooled dough one at a time, then stir in 40 g (1½ oz) of the grated cheese.

3. Add the dough to a piping bag with a medium-sized nozzle. Squeeze balls, about 3 cm (1¼ in) wide, onto a baking sheet lined with baking parchment. Sprinkle the balls with the remaining cheese and the poppy and sesame seeds.

4. Put the baking sheet in the oven, reduce the temperature to 180°C (350°F/gas 4) and bake the gougères for 20–22 minutes until golden brown. Remove from the heat and allow to cool.

PREPARATION TIME: about 35 minutes
BAKING TIME: 20–22 minutes · MAKES ABOUT 50

AT THE FOOT OF
THE EIFFEL TOWER

The 7th arrondissement is home to one of the city's most romantic parks – the **CHAMP DE MARS**. With its views of the **EIFFEL TOWER**, the **SEINE** and the **JARDINS DU TROCADÉRO** it is a popular meeting place for lovers from all over the world, and in good weather it is the ideal location for a culinary break.

The best place to stock up with ingredients for a picnic *à la parisienne* is one of the nearby markets, where as well as fantastic cheeses and fragrant baguettes you will also find fresh fruit and vegetables, delicious pâtés and marinated olives. If you want to spoil yourself, you can simply order a picnic basket and have it delivered to a secluded spot of your choice.

COQ au VIN BLANC

1 large **poularde** (approx. 1.5 kg/3 lb 5 oz, divided into eight pieces)

2 tbsp **olive oil**

1 heaped tbsp **plain (all-purpose) flour**

1 bottle of **dry white wine**

500 ml (17 fl oz/2 cups) **chicken stock**

1 large **onion**

1 large **carrot**

100 g (3½ oz) **celeriac (celery root)**

10 sprigs of **thyme**

2 **bay leaves**

300 g (10½ oz) small **bunched carrots**

250 g (9 oz) small **shallots**

100 g (3½ oz) **streaky bacon**

200 g (7 oz) small **field mushrooms**

30 g (1 oz) **butter**

1–2 pinches of **sugar**

salt and freshly ground **black pepper**

1. Rinse the poularde pieces in cold water and pat until completely dry. Heat the oil in a large roasting pan. Fry the poularde pieces – possibly in portions – all over for about 10 minutes until golden brown. Dust with the flour. Deglaze with a little of the wine, reduce, then pour in the remaining wine and the chicken stock, and bring to the boil. Peel and coarsely dice the onion, carrot and celeriac. Add the onion, carrot, celeriac, five sprigs of thyme and the bay leaf to the meat and stock, and season to taste with salt and pepper. Cook for 1 hour in a covered roasting pan over a low heat.

2. Meanwhile, wash the bunched carrots, leaving some of the leaves, and peel them. Lightly blanch the carrots in boiling salted water for about 2 minutes, then remove, rinse in cold water and drain. Peel the shallots. Cut the bacon into thin strips. Clean the mushrooms and rub dry with a dish towel. Heat the butter in a large saucepan and fry the shallots for about 8 minutes. Add the bacon and mushrooms and sauté for about 5 minutes. Season to taste with pepper, cover and keep warm.

3. Remove the poularde pieces from the sauce, cover and keep warm. Pass the sauce through a fine-meshed sieve and into a saucepan, thoroughly squeezing out the residue in the sieve. Pour the sauce and the mushroom mixture with stock into the roasting pan, bring to the boil and reduce slightly, until it is thick enough. Season to taste with salt, pepper and sugar. Add the poularde pieces and bunched carrots to the sauce, and heat for 5–10 minutes. Serve garnished with leaves from the remaining sprigs of thyme.

PREPARATION TIME: about 1 hour
COOKING TIME: about 1 hour
SERVES 4

GILT-HEAD BREAM
IN SALT CRUST

2 kg (4 lb 8 oz) coarse sea salt

2 egg whites

2 gilt-head bream (each about 600 g/1 lb 5 oz, ready
to cook)

1 organic lemon

1 garlic clove

4 sprigs of thyme

freshly ground black pepper

1. To make the salt crust, mix the sea salt with the egg whites and about 100 ml (3½ fl oz/scant ½ cup) of water in a large bowl to make a spreadable mixture. Distribute a third of the salt mixture over a baking sheet lined with baking parchment.

2. Preheat the oven to 200°C (400°F/gas 6). Thoroughly rinse the inside and outside of the gilt-head bream, and pat dry. Wash the lemon in hot water, pat dry and cut into thin slices. Peel and slice the garlic. Season the inside and outside of the fish with pepper, then stuff with the lemon, garlic and thyme and lay on the bed of salt. Spread the remaining salt mixture over the fish, and press together with moistened hands, so the fish are well coated. Put the baking sheet into the oven and cook the bream for 35 minutes.

3. To serve, remove the fish from the oven. Cut open the salt crust all the way round with a serrated knife in line with the dorsal fin, or break open and remove the 'lid'. Lift the bream out and fillet them.

PREPARATION TIME: about 30 minutes
COOKING TIME: 35 minutes
SERVES 4

73

MAIN COURSES · FISH & SEAFOOD

74

THE FIRST
KISS

At the border between the 8th and 17th arrondissements, surrounded by luxury Haussmann-style town houses, is the **PARC MONCEAU**. For sweethearts who have sauntered around the park, there is nothing better than sharing a beautifully scented crêpe at one of the stalls.

The singer Yves Duteil has even dedicated a *chanson* to the park. In *Au Parc Monceau*, he sings about the lake, the flowers and statues, the beauty, the calm and his first kiss.

JEAN RICHEPIN

THE ACACIA BRANCH

(extract)

[…]

With laugh and questioning look
Wouldst thou know
How many days I thee have loved.

Take then thyself a branch
From the acacia tree.

Take and break the branch
White with flowers less white than thee.

Pick one by one those flowers and leaves
And from those picked count and say how many
flowers and leaves
There be on all the acacia tree.

Since then I thee love
Now say thyself how many days there be.

[…]

77

BRIOCHES

1 cube of **fresh yeast** *(42 g / 1½ oz)*

550 g *(1 1lb 4 oz / 4½ cups)* **plain (all-purpose) flour**

75 g *(2½ oz / ⅓ cups)* **sugar**

1¼ tsp **salt**

1 tsp grated **organic lemon zest**

4 **cold eggs** *(medium)*

250 g *(9 oz)* **cold butter**

1 **egg yolk**

2 tbsp **milk**

Note: This recipe requires a non-fan-assisted oven.

78

1. The day before, finely crumble the yeast. Mix the flour, yeast, sugar, salt, lemon zest, eggs and 3 tablespoons of cold water for 5 minites in a food processor or using a hand-held mixer with a dough hook on a low setting. Cut the butter into small pieces and gradually knead it in. Knead the dough for about 10 minutes on a medium setting, until it looks silky and is elastic. Cover the bowl with a dish towel and leave the dough to rise in the fridge for at least 10 hours (or overnight).

2. The next day, thoroughly grease the moulds with butter. Briefly knead the dough by hand on a lightly floured work surface, and then break off 20 portions, each weighing about 50 g (2 oz). Roll each portion on a little flour to form a smooth ball. Form 20 small balls from the remaining dough. Put the large balls of dough in the moulds, press a deep hole in the middle of each one and put a small ball in each hole. Cover with a dish towel and leave to rise at room temperature for about 1½ hours, until the dough has risen to just below the edge of the mould.

3. Preheat the oven to 180°C (350°F/gas 4). Whisk the egg yolks and milk, and brush the brioches with the mixture. Bake in the oven for 18–20 minutes until golden yellow. Remove, briefly cool, then remove from the moulds and allow to cool on a cooling rack.

PREPARATION TIME: about 1 hour 30 minutes
RESTING TIME: at least 10 hours (or overnight)
BAKING TIME: 18–20 minutes
MAKES 20

TUNA
RILLETTE

300 g (10½ oz) tuna steak

200 ml (7 fl oz/scant 1 cup) fish stock

1 shallot

3–4 sprigs of tarragon

50 g (2 oz) soft butter

50 g (2 oz) crème fraîche

3 tsp grated organic lemon zest

*2–3 tbsp Noilly Prat
(dry white vermouth, optional)*

sea salt and freshly ground black pepper

8–12 slices of baguette

1 tbsp tarragon leaves

1. Cut the tuna into large pieces. Heat the fish stock in a frying pan (skillet), add the fish pieces, cover, then steep in the hot stock for 8 minutes. Remove the fish pieces and put the stock to one side. Allow the fish to cool slightly, then tear into small pieces in a bowl.

2. Peel and very finely dice the shallot. Rinse the tarragon, pat dry, pluck off the leaves and finely chop. Add the shallot, tarragon, 5 tablespoons of fish stock, flaked butter, crème fraîche and grated lemon zest to the fish and mix everything with a fork. Stir in the vermouth or a further 2–3 tablepsoons of fish stock, to make the rillette nice and creamy. Season to taste with sea salt and pepper, cover, and steep for at least 2 hours.

3. Just before serving, toast the baguette slices. Season the rillette with salt and pepper to taste, spread over the baguette slices and sprinkle with tarragon leaves and lemon peel.

PREPARATION TIME: about 30 minutes
RESTING TIME: 2 hours
SERVES 4-6

81

AMUSE-BOUCHES

TERRINE DE CAMPAGNE
WITH ONION CONFIT

FOR THE TERRINE

700 g (1 lb 9 oz) **lean pork**
(e.g. schnitzel)

200 g (7 oz) **chicken liver**

100 g (3½ oz) **unsalted bacon**

40 g (1½ oz) **pistachio kernels**
(unsalted)

large pinch of freshly grated
nutmeg

4 tbsp **cognac**

2 **shallots**

2 tsp **thyme leaves**

1 **egg** *(medium)*

approx. 125 g (4 oz) **streaky
bacon** *in thin slices*

*salt and freshly ground
black pepper*

FOR THE ONION CONFIT

500 g **red onions**

1½ tsp **black peppercorns**

½ tsp **coriander seeds**

5 **allspice berries**

2 **cloves**

2 tsp **thyme leaves**

2 tbsp **olive oil**

2 tbsp **butter**

150 g (5 oz/⅔ cup) **sugar**

3 tbsp **vinegar**

3 tbsp **red wine**

2–3 tbsp **crème de cassis**

salt

1. To make the terrine, the day before rinse the pork, pat dry and dice. Clean the chicken liver. Cut the bacon into thin strips. Portion by portion, chop everything up small in a food processor or using a large knife. Put the mixture in a bowl, add the pistachio kernels, 1½ tablespoons of salt, plenty of pepper, the nutmeg and cognac, and thoroughly mix the ingredients by hand. Cover with cling film (plastic wrap) and marinate in the fridge overnight.

2. The next day preheat the oven to 180°C (350°F/gas 4). Peel and finely dice the shallots. Add the shallots, thyme and egg to the meat mixture and thoroughly mix by hand. Line a terrine mould with aluminium foil so it projects over the sides. Add the meat mixture to the mould, press firmly and line with the bacon slices. Seal the mould well with the aluminium foil.

3. Place the terrine mould in the oven's drip pan. Pour in hot water until the mould is two-thirds immersed. Cook in the oven for 1¼ hours. Remove the terrine from the oven and allow to cool in the mould. Then allow the flavour to develop for 1–2 days in the fridge.

4. To make the onion confit, peel and halve the onions, then cut into slices. Finely pound the spices with a pestle and mortar. Heat the olive oil and butter in a saucepan, add the onions, spices and thyme and sweat over a medium heat for about 15 minutes, until the onions are lightly browned and soft. Stir in the sugar, vinegar and red wine, and with the lid off reduce everything for about 30 minutes until thick. Pour in the crème de cassis, bring to the boil and season the confit to taste with salt.

5. To serve, grip the foil and lift the terrine from the mould, then cut into slices. Serve with the onion confit.

PREPARATION TIME: about 45 minutes
MARINATING TIME: 12 hours (overnight)
COOKING TIME: 1 hour 15 minutes · RESTING TIME: 1–2 days
SERVES 10–12

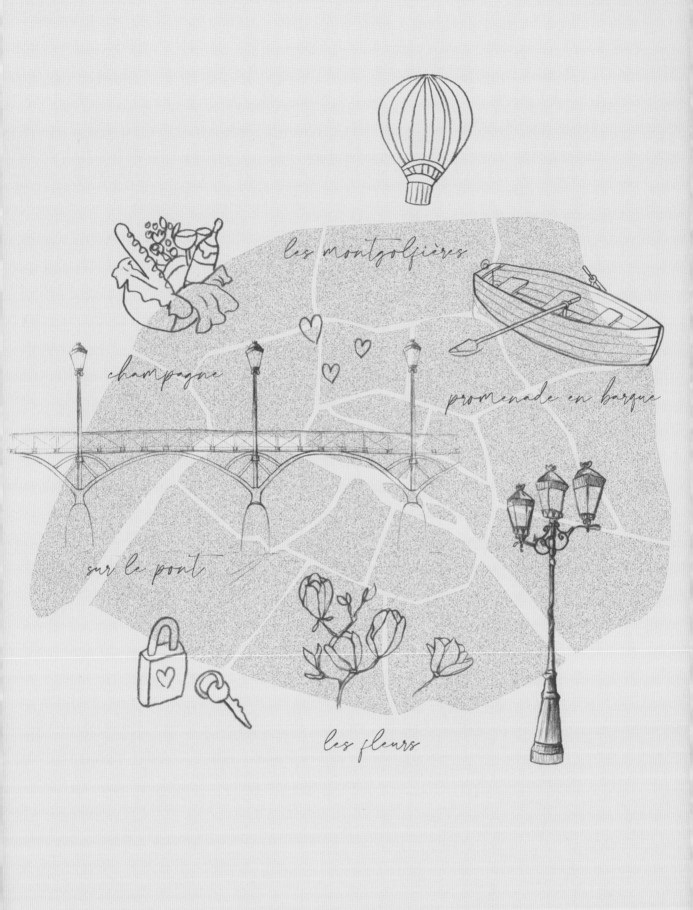

Paris

ALONG
THE SEINE

Anyone who has ever crossed one of the picturesque bridges over
the Seine, the water glittering in the evening sunlight,
knows why Paris is the world's most romantic city. No wonder it's
even said that kissing under the Pont Marie will make
your wishes come true …

88

FRENCH KISSING

The Seine is marvellous for couples – whether ambling together along the river bank, sipping a cup of coffee in one of the little riverside cafés or enjoying a boat trip. If you opt for the latter, you should make a wish under the **PONT MARIE** and kiss your beloved, as popular belief has it that the wish will then be fulfilled.

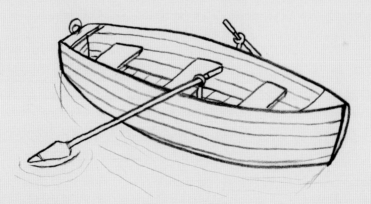

TOMATO SOUP
WITH TAPENADE

FOR THE SOUP

2.5 kg (5 lb 10 oz)
aromatic tomatoes

2 onions

2 garlic cloves

2 celery stalks

5 tbsp olive oil

2 bay leaves

4 tsp thyme leaves

about 600 ml (20 fl oz/2½ cups)
vegetable stock

2 heaped tbsp **tomato**
purée *(paste)*

1–2 pinches of **sugar**

salt and freshly ground
black pepper

FOR THE TAPENADE

150 g (5 oz) **aromatic black olives**
(unpitted)

1 tbsp **capers** *(from a jar)*

2 **anchovy fillets** *(marinated in*
oil or salt)

1–2 **garlic cloves**

6 tbsp **olive oil**

baguette

1. To make the soup, preheat the oven to 200°C (400°F/gas 6). Core and halve the tomatoes. Peel and coarsely chop the onions and garlic. Clean the celery and cut into slices 1 cm (½ in) thick. Mix the tomatoes with the olive oil, onions, garlic, celery, bay leaf and 2 teaspoons of thyme on a deep baking sheet. Season with a little salt and pepper. Cook the tomatoes in the oven for 1 hour.

2. Meanwhile, to make the tapenade, pit the olives, drain the capers, and rinse and pat dry the anchovies. Peel and coarsely chop the garlic. Finely purée the ingredients with the olive oil using a hand-held blender. Season to taste with pepper.

3. Transfer the tomatoes with the cooking liquid from the baking sheet to a saucepan, fishing out the bay leaves. Pour in the vegetable stock and add the tomato purée. Bring the soup to the boil, and continue to boil for 5 minutes with the lid off, then finely purée. Season to taste with the salt, pepper and sugar.

4. Ladle the soup into bowls, spoon in some tapenade, drizzle with a little olive oil, sprinkle with the remaining thyme leaves and pepper, and serve with slices of baguette.

PREPARATION TIME: 30 minutes
COOKING TIME: about 1 hour
SERVES 4

SOLE with BUTTER SAUCE

FOR THE SAUCE

175 g (6 oz) *cold butter*

1 *shallot*

2 tbsp *Noilly Prat*
(dry white vermouth)

125 ml (4 fl oz / ½ cup) **dry**
white wine

2 tbsp *white wine vinegar*

100 ml (3½ oz / ¾ cup) *fish stock*

FOR THE SOLE

1 *organic lemon*

½ bunch of *flat-leaf parsley*

4 *sole (ready to cook, without*
fins, skin and head, each about
350 g / 12 oz)

about 100 g (3½ oz / ¾ cup) **plain**
(all-purpose) flour

6 tbsp *clarified butter*

salt and freshly ground
black pepper

1. To make the sauce, apart from 1 tablespoon, cut the butter into small cubes and freeze for about 20 minutes. Meanwhile, peel and very finely dice the shallot. Froth up the 1 tablespoon of butter in a small saucepan, then sweat the diced shallot until translucent. Pour in the Noilly Prat, white wine, vinegar and fish stock, bring to the boil and reduce the liquid to a third over a high heat. Pass through a fine-meshed sieve into a second small saucepan, thoroughly squeezing out the residue in the sieve.

2. Preheat the oven to 150°C (300°F/gas 1). Peel the lemon and cut into thin slices. Rinse the parsley, pat dry, pluck off the leaves and very finely chop.

3. Rinse the sole in cold water, pat dry and season to taste with salt and pepper. Coat the fish in flour, patting off any excess. Heat the clarified butter in non-stick pans, fry the sole in it for 5 minutes over a medium heat, carefully turn (ideally with two spatulas), and sauté the other side for a further 3–5 minutes. Place the sole on a baking sheet lined with baking parchment, and put in the oven to keep warm.

4. Bring the wine jus to the boil, then reduce the heat and gradually stir the cold diced butter into the liquid with a sauce whisk, not allowing it to reboil, otherwise it will curdle! Season the jus with salt and pepper, then remove the saucepan from the heat.

5. Serve the sole on heated plates, garnish with slices of lemon, sprinkle with parsley and serve with the sauce.

PREPARATION TIME: about 50 minutes

SERVES 4

CHESTNUT VELOUTÉ

FOR THE SOUP

2 cloves

1 tsp coriander seeds

1 onion

*125 g (4 oz) celeriac
(celery root)*

1 tbsp butter

3 tbsp white wine

*about 1.2 litres (40 fl oz / 4¾ cups)
chicken or vegetable stock*

*400 g (14 oz) cooked chestnuts
(vacuum-packed)*

1 bay leaf

½ cinnamon stick

150 g (5 oz / ⅔ cup) crème fraîche

freshly grated nutmeg

*salt and freshly ground
black pepper*

FOR THE TOPPING

2 tbsp hazelnut kernels

1 tart apple

1 heaped tbsp butter

1 tbsp parsley leaves

1. Finely pound the cloves and coriander using a pestle and mortar. Peel and finely dice the onion and the celeriac. Froth up the butter in a saucepan and brown the pounded spices in it for 30–60 seconds, until they give off a fragrance. Add the onion and sweat until translucent. Add the celeriac, deglaze with the white wine, then pour in the chicken or vegetable stock. Put 2 tablespoons of chestnuts to one side, then add the remaining chestnuts, the bay leaf and the cinnamon to the saucepan. Bring to the boil, and continue to boil for 20 minutes, with the lid on.

2. Remove the bay leaf and cinnamon stick. Add 100 g (3½ oz / ½ cup)of the crème fraîche, bring the soup to the boil and finely purée with a hand-held blender. Season to taste with salt, pepper and nutmeg. Keep hot, with the lid on.

3. For the topping, coarsely chop the remaining chestnuts and the hazelnuts. Core the apple and cut into thin slices. Heat the butter in a pan. Add the apple, chestnuts and nuts and sauté for 2–3 minutes, tossing them now and again. Mix in the parsley leaves and remove the pan from the heat.

4. To serve, briefly reheat the soup, froth it up with a whisk and pour into bowls. Spoon over the remaining crème fraîche and the topping and serve.

PREPARATION TIME: about 20 minutes
COOKING TIME: about 20 minutes
SERVES 4

ETERNALLY YOURS, ETERNALLY MINE, ETERNALLY US

Until a few years ago an absolute must for all lovers was to attach a love lock to the **PONT DES ARTS** and cast the key into the Seine, as a sign of their enduring love. Even though the collapse of a section of bridge railing in 2014 has meant that attaching locks to the railing is no longer allowed, the bridge still attracts couples from all over the world. On balmy summer evenings they enjoy the special atmosphere, the buskers and the views of the **INSTITUT FRANÇAIS** and the **LOUVRE**, while imbibing a glass of red wine.

And time and again the bridge is a favourite film and TV location for avowals of love – for example, in the season finale of *Sex and the City* when Carrie and Mr Big meet on the Pont des Arts one evening and Mr Big declares to Carrie that she's The One.

MADELEINES

FOR THE BATTER

135 g (5 oz) **butter**

1 vanilla pod (bean)

3 eggs (medium)

125 g (4 oz/½ cup) **sugar**

25 g (1 oz) **liquid honey**

pinch of salt

150 g (5 oz/1¼ cups) **plain
(all-purpose) flour**

1 heaped tsp **baking powder**

1 tsp grated **organic lemon zest**

PLUS

soft butter and flour

icing (confectioner's) sugar

1. The day before, melt the butter for the batter and leave to cool until lukewarm. Cut open the vanilla pod lengthways and scrape out the seeds. In a bowl, beat the eggs, sugar, honey, vanilla seeds and salt using a hand-held mixer with a beater attachment, until the mixture is frothy and light yellow. Sieve the flour and baking powder into another bowl. Add the flour mixture, lukewarm butter and the grated lemon zest to the egg/sugar mixture, and stir to combine. Cover the bowl, and leave the batter to rest in the fridge for at least 12 hours, or overnight.

2. The next day preheat the oven to 220°C (430°F/gas 8). Thoroughly grease the madeleine tin, then dust with flour, patting off any excess. Spoon the batter into the depressions until they are two-thirds full. Bake the madeleines in the middle of the oven for 8–10 minutes until golden brown.

3. Remove from the oven, briefly cool, then flip the madeleines out of the depressions and allow to cool further on a cooling rack. Before baking any further madeleines, clean the tin, re-grease and dust with flour. Repeat the process with the remaining batter. Dust the cooled madeleines with icing sugar.

PREPARATION TIME: about 30 minutes
RESTING TIME: 12 hours (overnight) · **BAKING TIME**: 8–10 minutes
MAKES ABOUT 28

98

BAKERY ITEMS

OVEN-ROASTED
LEG OF LAMB

1 leg of lamb on the
bone (approx. 1.8 kg/4 lb)

3 tbsp olive oil

250 g (9 oz) shallots

1 fresh head of garlic

500 g (1 lb 2 oz) potatoes
(waxy)

250 g (9 oz) bunched carrots

3 parsley roots

1 leek

5 sprigs of rosemary

5 bay leaves

150 ml (5 fl oz/scant ⅔ cup) dry
red wine

400 ml (13 fl oz/generous 1½ cups)
lamb or beef stock

500 g (1 lb 2 oz) cherry tomatoes

sea salt and freshly ground black
pepper

1. Preheat the oven to 200°C (400°F/gas 6). Rinse the leg of lamb in cold water
and pat dry. Heat the olive oil in a wide roasting pan. Over a medium heat sear the
lamb all over for about 15 minutes until dark brown, season with sea salt and
pepper and roast uncovered in the oven for 45 minutes.

2. Meanwhile, peel the shallots, halving any large ones lengthways. Halve the
head of garlic crossways. Peel or thoroughly brush the potatoes and quarter them.
Peel the carrots and parsley roots, and cut into in large chunks. Clean the leek
thoroughly and cut into pieces about 5 cm (2 in) long. Rinse the rosemary and
pat dry.

3. Remove the lamb from the oven and turn it over. Lay the shallots, garlic,
potatoes, parsley roots, rosemary and bay leaves around the lamb in the roasting
juices and season to taste with sea salt and pepper. Add the wine and stock. Roast in
the oven for a further 30 minutes. Add the leek, carrots and tomatoes, and cook for
a further 45 minutes.

4. Remove the lamb from the roasting pan and rest for 10 minutes wrapped in
aluminium foil. Season the vegetables and sauce with sea salt and pepper. Slice the
lamb off the bone and serve with the vegetables and roasting juices.

PREPARATION TIME: about 30 minutes
COOKING TIME: about. 2 hours
SERVES 6-8

OYSTERS AU GRATIN
with MORNAY SAUCE

1 shallot
40 g (1½ oz) **gruyère**
2 tbsp **butter**

1 heaped tbsp **flour**
250 ml (8½ fl oz/1 cup) **milk**
freshly grated **nutmeg**

1–2 squeezes of fresh **lemon juice**
16 **oysters**
salt and freshly ground
black pepper

1. Peel and very finely dice the shallot. Finely grate the cheese. Heat the butter in a small saucepan, and sweat the diced shallot in it until translucent. Stir in the flour. Pour in the milk, stirring continuously, and heat, continuing to stir, until the sauce has thickened. Put aside 2 tablespoons of cheese, then stir the remaining cheese into the sauce and allow to melt. Remove the saucepan from the heat, season the sauce to taste with salt, pepper and nutmeg and add the lemon juice. Cover and put to one side.

2. Carefully open the oysters with a shucking knife, retaining the oyster water and passing it through a fine-meshed sieve. Remove the oysters from their shells and place on a plate. Rinse the lower shells, dry, replace the oysters and lay the shells on a baking sheet.

3. Preheat the oven grill (broiler). Heat the sauce, pour in the oyster water and stir in. Season the sauce to taste with salt, pepper and nutmeg. Pour a little sauce onto the oysters. Sprinkle with the remaining cheese. Grill for about 5 minutes, until the sauce is lightly browned. Remove and serve hot.

PREPARATION TIME: about 35 minutes
SERVES 4

102

AMUSE-BOUCHES

AN ISLAND
FOR LOVERS

Two of the city's greatest love stories start on the ÎLE DE LA CITÉ: the fateful romance between Héloïse and her teacher Abelard (see page 31) and Quasimodo's unrequited love for Esmeralda in Victor Hugo's world-famous novel *The Hunchback of Notre-Dame*.

If you'd rather write your own love story, you should wander through the winding alleys around the PLACE DAUPHINE, take a short break under the weeping willow on the SQUARE DU VERT-GALANT or cross the PONT-NEUF – the city's oldest bridge. The latter was one of the main locations for the French feature film *The Lovers on the Bridge*, in which the vagrant Alex and the sick Michèle fall in love with each other.

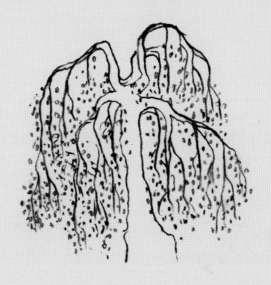

FILLET STEAK with CAFÉ DE PARIS SAUCE AND CHICORY

FOR THE MEAT AND THE CAFÉ DE PARIS SAUCE

1 anchovy fillet

1 tsp tarragon leaves

2 shallots

100 g (3½ oz) soft butter

1 tsp capers (from a jar)

1 tsp Dijon mustard

2 tbsp tomato ketchup

2 tsp cognac

1–2 drops of Worcestershire sauce

2 tbsp olive oil

4 beef tenderloin steaks – centre cuts (each about 175 g/6 oz)

100 ml (3½ fl oz/scant ½ cup) cream

salt and freshly ground black pepper

FOR THE CHICORY

6 medium-sized chicory heads

1 tbsp butter

1 tbsp sugar

1 tbsp tarragon vinegar

100 ml (3½ fl oz/scant ½ cup) chicken stock

100 ml (3½ fl oz/scant ½ cup) single (light) cream

1. To make the Café de Paris sauce, rinse the anchovy fillet and pat dry. Finely chop the tarragon. Peel and dice the shallots. Use a hand-held blender to finely purée the butter, anchovy, tarragon, shallots, capers, mustard, ketchup and cognac in a mixing jug. Add the Worcestershire sauce and season to taste with salt and pepper.

2. Cut off the ends of the chicory heads so they stay in one piece, removing any limp leaves. Heat the butter in a large saucepan, and over a medium to high heat thoroughly cook both sides of the chicory for 1–2 minutes. Sprinkle over the sugar, and briefly caramelise. Deglaze with the vinegar, and add the chicken stock and cream. Cover the pan, and gently simmer the chicory heads over a low heat for about 15 minutes, or until soft, turning them over halfway through the cooking time. Make sure there is sufficient liquid in the pan, and if necessary add 1–2 tablespoons of water.

3. Meanwhile, heat the oil for the steaks in a second pan, and over a medium heat sear both sides for 2–3 minutes, then season to taste with salt and pepper. Remove the steaks, wrap in aluminium foil and allow to rest for 5 minutes.

4. Heat the Café de Paris sauce in a small saucepan, pour in the cream and froth up well using a hand-held blender. Serve the steaks with the sauce and the chicory.

PREPARATION TIME: about 45 minutes
SERVES 4

VICTOR HUGO

THE HUNCHBACK OF NOTRE-DAME

(extract)

On the following morning she perceived on awaking that she had been asleep. This singular thing astonished her. She had been so long unaccustomed to sleep! A joyous ray of the rising sun entered through her window and touched her face.

At the same time, at that window she beheld together with the sun an object which frightened her, the unfortunate face of Quasimodo. She involuntarily closed her eyes again, but in vain; she fancied that she still saw through the rosy lids that gnome's mask, one-eyed and gap-toothed. Then, while keeping her eyes closed, she heard a rough voice saying, very gently, 'Be not afraid. I am your friend. I came to watch you sleep. It does not hurt you if I come to see you sleep, does it? What difference does it make to you if I am here when your eyes are closed! Now I am going. Stay, I have placed myself behind the wall. You can open your eyes again.'

There was something more plaintive than these words, and that was the accent in which they were uttered. The gypsy, much touched, opened her eyes. He was, in fact, no longer at the window. She approached the opening, and beheld the poor hunchback crouching in an angle of the wall, in a sad and resigned attitude. She made an effort to surmount the repugnance with which he inspired her.

'Come,' she said to him gently.

From the movement of the gypsy's lips, Quasimodo thought that she was driving him away; then he rose and retired, limping slowly and with drooping head, without even daring to raise to the young girl his gaze full of despair.

'Do come,' she cried, but he continued to retreat. Then she darted from her cell, ran to him, and grasped his arm. On feeling her touch him Quasimodo trembled in every limb. He raised his suppliant eye, and seeing that she was leading him back to her quarters his whole face beamed with joy and tenderness.

SPRING SALAD
WITH SCALLOPS

250 g (9 oz) *green asparagus*

1 small *fennel*

½ bunch of *radishes*

½ bunch of *chives*

½ bunch of *chervil*

3 tbsp juice and the zest of 1 *organic lemon*

1 tsp *maple syrup*

6 tbsp *finest olive oil*

12 *scallops*

1 tbsp *flour*

1 tbsp *olive oil*

1 tbsp *butter*

sea salt and freshly ground *black pepper*

1. Wash the asparagus, cut off the ends and peel the bottom third of the shoots. Cut the asparagus diagonally into thin slices. Clean the fennel, trim off the stalks and cut into thin slices. Clean the radishes, put eight of them aside and cut the remainder into fine slices. Rinse the chives and chervil, and pat dry. Cut the chives into small rings and pluck off the chervil leaves. Mix the ingredients in a bowl to make a salad.

2. To make the vinaigrette, vigorously whisk the lemon juice and zest, maple syrup and olive oil, and a little salt and pepper to taste.

3. Rinse the scallops in cold water and pat well until dry. Thinly dust with flour, patting off any excess. Heat the oil and butter in a frying pan (skillet), cook the scallops over a medium heat for 3 minutes until light brown, then season with salt and pepper. Remove the pan from the heat.

4. Serve the salad, whole radishes and scallops and drizzle with the vinaigrette.

PREPARATION TIME: about 40 minutes
SERVES 4

PISTACHIO FINANCIERS

880 g (1 lb 15 oz) **green pistachio kernels**
(unsalted, unroasted)
125 g (4 oz) **butter**
150 g (5 oz/1¼ cups) **icing (confectioner's)**
sugar
50 g (2 oz/⅓ cup) **plain (all-purpose) flour**
100 g (3½ oz) **egg white** *(from 3 medium eggs)*

112

1. Prepare the batter the day before. To do so, finely chop the pistachio kernels in a food processor or blender. Melt the butter in a small saucepan and let it go a nutty brown. Cool until lukewarm. Stir the icing sugar, flour and pistachios in a bowl. Stir in the butter, then the egg whites. Add the batter to a piping bag with a nozzle, and rest in the fridge for several hours or overnight.

2. The next day, preheat the oven to 220°C (430°F/gas 8). Metal tins should be thoroughly coated with melted butter, while silicone moulds don't need greasing. Add the batter to just under the edge of the depressions and bake the financiers until golden brown (the time will depend on the size of the moulds or tins you use). In small moulds/tins, the batter needs about 8 minutes' baking time, and in larger depressions or a muffin tin, 10–15 minutes. Remove from the oven, briefly cool, remove the financiers from the moulds/tins and allow to cool on a cooling rack. Repeat the process with the remaining batter.

PREPARATION TIME: about 20 minutes
RESTING TIME: overnight · **BAKING TIME:** 8–15 minutes
FOR 36 VERY SMALL
OR 12 LARGER FINANCIERS

BAKERY ITEMS

VICHYSSOISE

FOR THE SOUP

1 onion

1 garlic clove

2 medium-sized *leeks*

1 celery stalk

300 g (10½ oz) *potatoes (floury)*

50 g (2 oz) *butter*

about 1 litre (34 fl oz/4 cups) **chicken**
or **vegetable stock**

freshly grated **nutmeg**

1–2 squeezes of fresh **lemon juice**

salt and freshly ground
black pepper

½ bunch of **chives**

100 g (3½ oz/½ cup) **crème fraîche**

1. Peel and finely dice the onion and garlic. Wash the leeks thoroughly, and cut just the white parts into thin rings; use the green parts for something else, such as a vegetable stock. Wash the celery and cut into thin slices. Peel and finely dice the potatoes.

2. Froth the butter in a saucepan and sweat the onion, garlic, leeks and celery. Pour in the chicken or vegetable stock and add the potatoes. Bring to the boil, and continue to boil for about 20 minutes, until the vegetables are nice and soft. Purée the soup with a hand-held blender, and season to taste with the salt, pepper and nutmeg and add the lemon juice. Allow the soup to cool, then keep refrigerated until you are ready to serve.

3. Shortly before serving, rinse the chives, pat dry and cut into small rings. Season the cold soup to taste with salt, pepper and nutmeg, pour into bowls, spoon a little crème fraîche on top and sprinkle with the chives.

PREPARATION TIME: about 35 minutes plus cooling time
SERVES 4

113

PARIS IS AT ITS MOST BEAUTIFUL WHEN IT RAINS

Gil Pender is of this opinion in the film *Midnight in Paris*. For him, sauntering through the city of love in the rain is pure poetry. At the end of the film, he strolls across the **PONT ALEXANDRE III** and once again encounters the antiques dealer Gabrielle, at whose shop he bought a Cole Porter record a few days before. The two of them establish that they are of the same opinion, and Gil accompanies the beautiful Gabrielle home in the rain.

The opulent bridge is also a popular meeting place for lovers at sunset, as it offers a spectacular view of the **EIFFEL TOWER** and the **GRAND PALAIS**. Small wonder people like using it as a backdrop for marriage proposals.

CHERRY GALETTE

FOR THE PASTRY DOUGH

*250 g (9 oz/2 cups) plain
(all-purpose) flour*

3 tbsp sugar

¼ tsp salt

110 g cold butter

*50 g (2 oz/¼ cup)
crème fraîche*

FOR THE TOPPING

*600 g (1 lb 5 oz) fresh
sour cherries*

2 tbsp sugar

1 tbsp cornflour (cornstarch)

*2 tbsp ground almonds
(almond meal)*

2 tbsp milk

2 tbsp flaked (slivered) almonds

*200 g (7 oz/scant 1 cup)
crème fraîche*

icing (confectioner's) sugar

1. To make the pastry dough, rub together the flour, sugar, salt, butter in small flakes and crème fraîche to form a coarse crumb. Add 2–3 tablespoons of ice-cold water, and quickly knead to form a dough. The dough must not be over-kneaded – small, about pea-sized pieces of butter should still be visible, to make the pastry nice and crumbly. Wrap in cling film (plastic wrap) and refrigerate for 1 hour.

2. Meanwhile, wash, drain and pit the cherries. Mix in a bowl with the sugar and starch, and allow them to steep in the juice.

3. Preheat the oven to 220°C (430°F/gas 8). Roll the pastry out on a little flour to form a round (about 32 cm/12½ in in diameter), and lay on a baking sheet lined with baking parchment. Sprinkle the pastry base with the ground almonds. Spread the cherries over the pastry base, leaving a border of about 4 cm (1½ in). Loosely fold the border over the cherries, brush with the milk and sprinkle with the flaked almonds.

4. Bake the galette for 30–35 minutes on the lowest shelf of the oven, until the pastry is well browned. Remove, sprinkle icing sugar over the pastry border and serve the galette either straight from the oven or cooled (until lukewarm), together with the crème fraîche.

PREPARATION TIME: about 40 minutes
RESTING TIME: 1 hour · **BAKING TIME:** 30–35 minutes
SERVES 6-8

MELON SALAD
WITH HAM AND
BASIL

*1 large ripe **Charentais** or*
cantaloupe melon

2 shallots

*8–12 thin slices of **raw ham***
(e.g. jambon de Bayonne)

*2 tbsp **sherry vinegar***

*1 tbsp **balsamic vinegar***

*6 tbsp **finest** olive oil*

***purple** and green*
basil leaves

sea salt
*and freshly ground **black pepper***

1 baguette

1. Halve the melon, remove the seeds, cut into thin slices and peel. Peel the shallots and cut into very fine slices. Arrange the melon slices and ham on four plates, and top with the sliced shallots.

2. For the vinaigrette, mix both vinegars with a little sea salt and pepper, then stir in the oil. Drizzle the melon slices and ham with the vinaigrette, and sprinkle with the basil leaves. Serve with slices of baguette.

PREPARATION TIME: about 20 minutes
SERVES 4

PETITS POTS
DE CRÈME

1 vanilla pod (bean)
300 ml (10 fl oz/1¼ cups) **milk**
200 ml (7 fl oz/scant 1 cup) **cream**
5 **egg yolks** *(medium)*
80 g (3 oz/⅓ cup) **sugar**
approx. 250 g (9 oz) **mixed berries**
1–2 tbsp **icing (confectioner's) sugar** *(optional)*

1. Slit open the vanilla pod lengthways and scrape out the seeds. Heat the milk, cream, vanilla seeds and pod in a saucepan. Briefly mix the egg yolks and sugar, using a hand-held mixer with a beater attachment, until the sugar has dissolved. Pour the hot vanilla milk through a sieve over the egg/sugar mixture, while stirring continuously. Scoop the foam off the surface, and pour the egg/milk mixture into four or six ramekins or ovenproof glasses.

2. Preheat the oven to 140°C (275°F/gas ½). Place the ramekins or glasses in a wide gratin dish, and pour in hot water until they are two-thirds immersed. Put the dish on the middle shelf of the oven and cook for 45 minutes. Remove the ramekins/glasses from the water, cool, then cover and refrigerate for at least 4 hours.

3. Check the berries, wash if necessary, and cut any strawberries smaller. Mix the berries, sprinkle with icing sugar to taste, and leave for a while to allow juice to develop. To serve, spoon the berries over the cream pots.

PREPARATION TIME: about 30 minutes
COOKING TIME: 45 minutes · **COOLING TIME:** 4 hours
SERVES 4-6

PARISIAN ONION SOUP

750 g (1 lb 10 oz) **brown onions**

3 tbsp **butter**

2 tbsp **flour**

125 ml (4 fl oz/½ cup) **dry white wine**

approx. 1.5 litres (50 fl oz/6 cups) **beef stock**

1 **bay leaf**

1 tbsp **thyme leaves**

8–12 slices of **baguette**

150 g (5 oz) strong **gruyère** *or* **Alpine cheese**

sea salt

cayenne pepper

freshly grated **nutmeg**

1. Peel the onions and cut into thin rings. Heat the butter in a large saucepan. Over a low heat slowly sweat the onions for about 15 minutes, until they are golden brown and soft, stirring occasionally.

2. Dust the onions with the flour and stir in. Deglaze with the white wine. Add the stock, bay leaf and thyme. Bring the soup to the boil, and continue to simmer for 20 minutes, uncovered. Season well with salt, cayenne pepper and nutmeg, and remove the bay leaf.

3. Briefly toast both sides of the baguette slices under the grill until golden brown. Preheat the oven to 250°C (475°F/gas 9). Coarsely grate the cheese. Spoon the soup into four heat-resistant soup bowls, lay the slices of toasted baguette on the soup and sprinkle with the cheese. Bake in the oven for about 2 minutes until golden yellow, and serve immediately.

PREPARATION TIME: about 15 minutes
COOKING TIME: about 35 minutes
SERVES 4

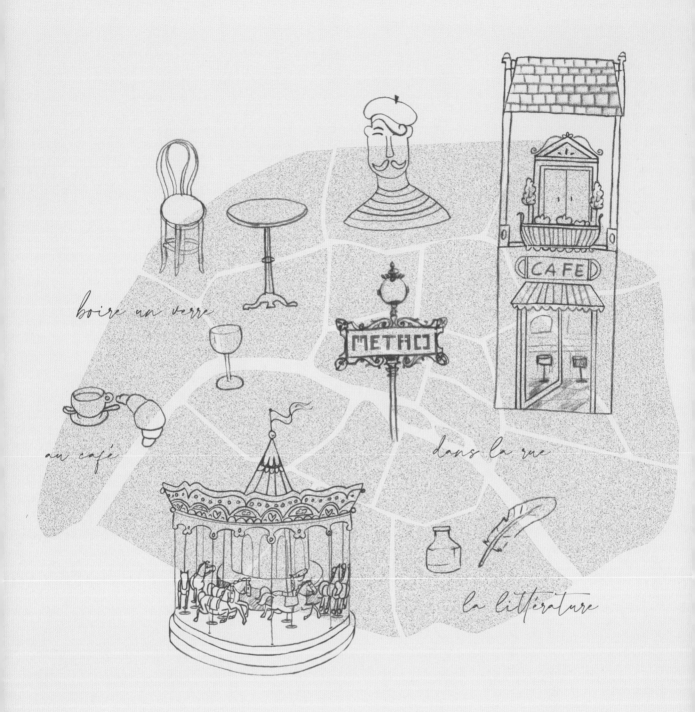

boire un verre

au café

METRO

dans la rue

CAFE

la littérature

Paris

ON THE STREETS

Le savoir-vivre is the art of enjoying life.
Wandering through Parisian alleys together or sipping a
glass of wine in a cosy bistro, we can experience it with all
our senses.

AN AMERICAN
AND HIS LOVE
FOR PARIS

Hardly anyone has managed to express their deep love for the city on the Seine as well as Ernest Hemingway. His posthumously published book *A Moveable Feast* is a declaration of love for Paris – the city, the people, the joie de vivre and the eccentric literary scene of the twenties.

Why not visit one of his favourite cafés and experience the enchantment of the places where Hemingway found his inspiration and met with other writers of his day? Try the **CAFÉ DE FLORE** and **LES DEUX MAGOTS** in **SAINT-GERMAIN-DES-PRÉS**. The latter even gets a mention in his book *Fiesta*, which he largely wrote at **LA CLOSERIE DES LILAS**. Incidentally, at this café in Montparnasse he also first read the manuscript of F. Scott Fitzgerald's novel *The Great Gatsby*.

So just get out there! Because according to Hemingway there are only two places where you can live happily: at home and in Paris.

TARTINES
WITH SAUTÉED
MUSHROOMS

FOR THE HERB CREAM

½ bunch of *flat-leaf parsley*

1 ripe *avocado*

1 *garlic clove*

100 g (3½ oz / ½ cup) *crème fraîche*

1–2 tsp fresh *lime juice*

salt and freshly ground

black pepper

FOR THE MUSHROOMS

400 g (14 oz) *mushrooms*
(e.g. champignons or king oyster)

1 *shallot*

1 tbsp *olive oil*

2 tbsp *butter*

2 tsp *thyme leaves*

1 tbsp *parsley leaves*

2–3 large slices of
sourdough bread

1. To make the herb cream, rinse the parsley, pat dry and pluck off the leaves. Halve the avocado and remove the stone. Peel and coarsely chop the garlic. Use a hand-held blender to finely purée the parsley, avocado flesh, garlic, crème fraîche and lime juice. Season the herb cream to taste with salt and pepper.

2. Clean the mushrooms, rub with a dish towel and cut into thick slices. Peel and finely dice the shallot. In a saucepan, heat the oil and butter, and sauté the mushrooms and shallot for about 5 minutes over a medium heat. Fold in the thyme and season with salt and pepper. Remove the pan from the heat.

3. Chop the parsley leaves. Toast the slices of bread until crispy. Spread the herb cream over the slices of toast, arrange the mushrooms on top and sprinkle with the parsley. Cut the toast into pieces and serve.

PREPARATION TIME: about 25 minutes
SERVES 4

135

AMUSE-BOUCHES

BŒUF BOURGUIGNON

1 kg (2 lb 4 oz) *marbled beef*
(suitable for braising, e.g.
silverside)

3 *garlic cloves*

2 *onions*

3 *sprigs of* **thyme**

3 **bay leaves**

1 *bottle of* **red wine**

(preferably Burgundy)

2 *carrots*

3 tbsp **oil**

1 *heaped tbsp* **flour**

500 ml (17 fl oz/4 cups) **beef stock**

250 g (9 oz) small **shallots**

100 g (3½ oz) **streaky bacon**

250 g (9 oz) small **field**
mushrooms

30 g (1 oz) **butter**

1 tbsp **sugar**

salt and freshly ground
black pepper

1. The evening before, cut the meat into about 6 cm (2½ in) cubes and put in a bowl. Peel and finely chop the garlic. Peel the onions, coarsely dice and mix with the garlic, thyme, bay leaf and beef in a bowl. Pour in the red wine and mix everything well. Cover the bowl and marinate the beef in the fridge overnight.

2. The next day, remove the beef from the marinade, drain and pat dry. Peel and coarsely dice the carrots. Heat the oil in a roasting pan, and sauté the beef over a high heat for a few minutes, until well browned all over. Add the carrots, sprinkle over the flour and deglaze with a little of the marinade. Pour in the remaining marinade and the beef stock, season to taste with salt and pepper and bring to the boil. Cover the roasting pan and simmer for 2 hours 30 minutes. Pierce with a carving fork. If the fork is easy to pull out, the beef is cooked, otherwise braise the beef for a further 30 minutes or so.

3. Meanwhile, peel the shallots, cut the bacon into thin slices, clean the mushrooms and rub with a dish towel. Heat the butter in a saucepan and fry the shallots for about 8 minutes, until golden yellow. Sprinkle the sugar and briefly caramelise. Add the bacon and mushrooms, and fry for 5–8 minutes.

4. As soon as the beef is cooked, remove the pieces from the sauce, cover and keep warm. Fold the mushroom/bacon mixture together with the cooking juices into the sauce. Reduce the sauce for a few minutes, until it has thickened a little, then season with salt and pepper to taste. Return the beef to the sauce, and serve.

PREPARATION TIME: about 45 minutes
MARINATING TIME: 12 hours (overnight)
COOKING TIME: 2 hours 30 minutes
SERVES 4

TART
with SPINACH and GOAT'S CHEESE

750 g (1 lb 10 oz) fresh **spinach**

1 **onion**

2 **garlic cloves**

1 tbsp **butter**

freshly grated **nutmeg**

1 tsp **grated organic lemon zest**

4 **eggs** (medium)

250 g (9 oz/1 cup) **crème fraîche**

1 pack (280 g/10 oz) of **puff-pastry rounds** (refrigerated)

200 g (7 oz) **goat's-cheese roll**

2 tbsp **breadcrumbs**

salt and freshly ground black pepper

1. Wash the spinach and drain well. Peel and finely dice the onion and garlic. Heat the butter in a large saucepan, then sweat the onion until translucent. Add the garlic and briefly sweat with the onion. Add the spinach – still slightly wet – and briefly heat, until it collapses. Tip the contents of the saucepan into a sieve and drain, then transfer to a bowl and season to taste with salt, pepper and nutmeg and the grated lemon zest. Stir in the eggs and crème fraîche, and season with salt and pepper.

2. Preheat the oven to 220°C (430°F/gas 8). Take the puff pastry out of the fridge and bring to room temperature for 5 minutes. Cut the cheese into 12 slices. Roll out the pastry, lay it in the flan tin, lined with baking parchment, and prick the base several times with a fork. Sprinkle with breadcrumbs. Spread the spinach filling over the top, pour on the egg mixture and lay the slices of goat's cheese on top. Bake the tart on the lowest shelf of the oven for 25–30 minutes, until golden brown and crispy.

PREPARATION TIME: about 30 minutes

BAKING TIME: 25–30 minutes

SERVES 4-6

TO A PASSER-BY

(extract from The Flowers of Evil)

Around me thundered the deafening noise of the street,
In mourning apparel, portraying majestic distress,
With queenly fingers, just lifting the hem of her dress,
A stately woman passed by with hurrying feet.

Agile and noble, with limbs of perfect poise,
Ah, how I drank, thrilled through like a being insane,
In her look a dark sky, whence springs forth the hurricane,
There lay but the sweetness that charms, and the joy that destroys.

A flash – then the night ... O loveliness fugitive!
Whose glance has so suddenly caused me again to live,
Shall I not see you again till this life is o'er?

Elsewhere, far away ... too late, perhaps never more,
For I know not whither you fly, nor you where I go,
O soul that I would have loved, and that you know!

139

CANELÉS DE BORDEAUX

½ *vanilla pod (bean)*

20 g (¾ oz) *butter*

330 ml (11¼ fl oz / 1⅓ cups)
full-fat milk

135 g (5 oz / ⅔ cup) *sugar*

80 g (3 oz / ⅔ cup) *plain
(all-purpose) flour*

2 *egg yolks* (medium)

3 tbsp **dark rum**

1. The day before, slit open the vanilla pod lengthways and scrape out the seeds
for the batter. Melt the butter and leave to cool until lukewarm. Bring the milk and
vanilla pod to the boil in a saucepan, then pour the vanilla milk into a bowl. Allow
to cool for 5 minutes. Add the sugar and flour to the vanilla milk, stirring
constantly. If lumps have formed, pour the mixture through a fine-meshed sieve.
Stir in the egg yolks, then add the lukewarm butter and the rum and mix everything
thoroughly. The mixture will now have the consistency of a thin pancake batter.
Cover the bowl and refrigerate overnight.

2. The next day, preheat the oven to 240°C (475°F/gas 9). If you are using metal
moulds, brush them thoroughly with melted butter (silicone moulds do not need
greasing). Pour the batter into the moulds so each one is about two-thirds full. Place
the canelés on the middle shelf of the oven and bake for 8 minutes. Turn the oven
down to 180°C (350°F/gas 6) and bake the canelés for a further 45–50 minutes,
until crispy and well browned. Remove the canelés from the oven and allow to cool
for 5 minutes. Then flip them out of the moulds and leave to cool on a cooling rack.

TIP: The canelés will stay fresh for about three days in a tightly sealed container.

PREPARATION TIME: about 30 minutes
COOLING TIME: overnight · **BAKING TIME**: 50–55 minutes
MAKES 8

A KISS
IN THE HEART
OF THE CITY

One of the most popular *quartiers* for couples is the MARAIS — a wonderful part of the city for ambling hand in hand along the narrow alleys, admiring the proud old mansions. The most romantic alley, though, is without a shadow of doubt the RUE DES BARRES. With its bistros and cobblestones, it resembles a magical film set.

A setting no less beautiful is the area in front of the City Hall, which was the location for perhaps the world's most famous photograph — Robert Doisneau's *Kiss*. If you wish to re-enact this passionate moment, you should make your way to the HÔTEL DE VILLE.

RACK OF LAMB
WITH OLIVE CRUST AND
GREEN BEANS

FOR THE RACK OF LAMB

75 g (2½ oz) stale **white bread**

1 tbsp **pine nuts**

1 **shallot**

2 **garlic cloves**

50 g (2 oz) **butter**

4 stems of **flat-leaf parsley**

2–3 sprigs of **thyme**

20 **black olives**, drained

1 tsp grated **organic lemon zest**

1 **egg** (medium)

2 tbsp **olive oil**

2 **racks of lamb** (each about 400 g/14 oz, ready to cook)

salt and freshly ground **black pepper**

FOR THE VEGETABLES

600 g (1 lb 5 oz) **fine green beans**

3 **tomatoes**

2–3 sprigs of **summer savoury**

2 **shallots**

2 **garlic cloves**

2 tbsp **olive oil**

250 ml (8½ fl oz/1 cup) **vegetable stock**

1. To make the crust, grind down the white bread in a food processor. Coarsely chop the pine nuts. Peel and finely dice the shallots and garlic. Heat the butter in a saucepan and sweat the shallots and garlic until translucent, then add to the breadcrumbs along with the butter. Rinse the herbs, pat dry and pluck off the leaves. Finely chop the olives and herbs, and add to the breadcrumbs with the grated lemon zest, egg and pine nuts. Mix thoroughly with a fork, and season to taste with salt and pepper.

2. For the green bean mix, wash the beans and cut off the stems. Halve any long beans and cook in boiling salted water for 7–10 minutes until al dente, then rinse through a sieve until cold and drain. Wash and quarter the tomatoes, cut off the stems, remove the flesh and cut into small cubes. Rinse the summer savoury, pat dry and finely chop the leaves. Peel and finely chop the shallots and garlic.

3. For the lamb, preheat the oven to 160°C (320°F/gas 2). Heat the olive oil in a large frying pan (skillet). Sear the racks of lamb for 2–3 minutes, then remove and lay on a baking sheet. Season with salt and pepper. Coat the fatty side with the olive mixture and gently press in. Roast the lamb in the oven for 15–20 minutes, then remove and cover with aluminium foil to keep it warm. Preheat the grill (broiler) in the oven until hot.

144

4. Meanwhile, heat the olive oil in a large saucepan for the vegetables. Sweat the shallots and garlic until translucent. Pour in the vegetable stock, add the beans, tomatoes and summer savoury, heat for about 5 minutes and season with salt and pepper. Cover to keep the vegetables warm.

5. Grill the racks of lamb under the hot oven grill for 3–5 minutes, until golden brown. Remove, cover and allow to rest for a while, then cut the lamb into sections two bones wide, and serve with the bean mixture.

PREPARATION TIME: about 1 hour 15 minutes
SERVES 4

145

ZANDER FILLETS
WITH CHANTERELLE RAGOUT

FOR THE CHANTERELLE RAGOUT

600 g (1 lb 5 oz) *chanterelles*

2 *shallots*

2 tbsp *butter*

5 tbsp *white wine*

100 ml (3½ fl oz/scant ½ cup) *vegetable stock*

200 ml (7 fl oz/scant 1 cup) *single (light) cream*

1 tbsp *thyme leaves*

salt and freshly ground black pepper

FOR THE POTATOES

750 g (1 lb 10 oz) *potatoes (preferably waxy)*

2–3 tbsp *olive oil*

FOR THE FISH

4 *zander fillets with skin (each about 150 g/5 oz)*

2 tbsp *flour*

3 tbsp *olive oil*

1 tbsp *butter*

1. To make the ragout, clean the mushrooms, thoroughly brushing and wiping them (if they are very dirty, quickly run under cold water and then immediately pat dry). Peel and finely dice the shallots. Heat the butter in a saucepan and sweat the diced shallots until translucent. Add the mushrooms and briefly sauté. Deglaze with the white wine, pour in the stock and bring to the boil. Add the cream, bring back to the boil, season to taste with salt and pepper and considerably reduce for about 5 minutes, until the sauce has thickened. Stir in the thyme, then cover and keep warm.

2. Meanwhile, peel the potatoes and cut into cubes a good 1 cm (½ in) in size. Heat the olive oil in a frying pan (skillet), and over a medium heat fry the potato cubes for about 10 minutes, until golden brown, seasoning with salt and pepper.

3. Rinse the zander fillets in cold water and pat dry. With a sharp knife score them several times on the skin side. Season the fillets with salt and pepper, and thinly dust with flour, patting off any excess. Heat the olive oil in a large frying pan. First fry the fillets for 3–4 minutese skin side down over a medium heat, then turn and fry for a further 4 minutes. Add the butter and froth up once.

4. Briefly reheat the mushroom ragout and potatoes if necessary, then serve with the zander fillets.

PREPARATION TIME: about 1 hour
SERVES 4

A JOURNEY INTO
THE PAST

In the picturesque **QUARTIER LATIN** is a bookshop with a special history involving two people's love of books.

In 1919 the American émigrée Sylvia Beach opened her bookshop **SHAKESPEARE & COMPANY** in the Rue de l'Odéon. The shop became a meeting place for many writers, including Ernest Hemingway, F. Scott Fitzgerald and James Joyce. During the German occupation, however, the original business had to shut down, and it never reopened.

In 1964 the American George Whitman changed the name of his own bookshop from **LE MISTRAL** to Shakespeare & Company, in honour of his heroine Sylvia Beach. Within a very short time this bookshop was also attracting writers from all over the world. The owner had set himself the task of supporting artists. Consequently, to this very day, you can spend the night between the shop's bookshelves free of charge – the only requirement being that you read a book a day, help out in the shop for a few hours and leave a short one-page biography.

This bookshop, full of nooks and crannies, boasts shelves that are full right up to the ceiling, accommodating a varied collection of secondhand books. And once you have found your personal gem, you can immediately immerse yourself in the new book in the adjoining café.

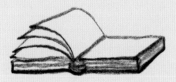

MINI
CROQUES-MADAME

100 g (3½ oz) strong **Alpine cheese**
(e.g. Comté)

3 tbsp **butter**

¼ bunch **chives**

2 thick slices of **white bread**

2–3 slices of **raw ham**

80 g (3 oz / ⅓ cup) **crème fraîche**

8 **quail's eggs**

sea salt and freshly ground **black pepper**

1. Preheat the oven to 240°C (475°F/gas 9). Finely grate the cheese. Melt 2 tablespoons of the butter. Rinse the chives, pat dry and cut into small rings.

2. Brush one side of the slices of bread with melted butter. Cut each slice into four, and lay on a baking sheet lined with baking parchment. Toast in the oven for 2–4 minutes until golden brown. Remove the bread from the oven, turn over and sprinkle with half the cheese.

3. Tear the ham into small pieces, lay on the toasted bread and put a spoonful of crème fraîche on top. Sprinkle with the remaining cheese. Bake the bread for about 5 minutes, until the cheese has melted and is lightly browned. Meanwhile, heat the remaining tablespoon of butter in a large frying pan (skillet) and fry the quail's eggs for 1–2 minutes.

4. Remove the bread from the oven and put a fried egg on each slice. Season with salt and pepper, sprinkle with chives and serve immediately.

PREPARATION TIME: about 20 minutes
SERVES 4

CONFIT OF COD
ON RATATOUILLE

FOR THE FISH

*4 cod fillets
(each approx. 175 g / 6 oz)*

2 red chilli peppers

*600 ml (20 fl oz / 2½ cups)
olive oil*

3 bay leaves

*5 cm (2 in) piece of organic
lemon peel*

sea salt

smoked paprika

FOR THE RATATOUILLE

1 red sweet (bell) pepper

1 yellow sweet (bell) pepper

1 small courgette (zucchini)

½ aubergine (eggplant)

1 shallot

2–3 garlic cloves

6 tbsp olive oil

2 tsp thyme leaves

*salt and freshly ground
black pepper*

1. For the fish, preheat the oven to 100°C (210°F/gas ½). Rinse the cod fillets in cold water and thoroughly pat dry. Halve the chilli peppers lengthways. Put the oil, chilli halves, bay leaves and lemon peel into an ovenproof dish and cook in the oven for 15 minutes. Lay the cod fillets in the hot oil – the oil must completely cover them. Cook in the oven for 25 minutes.

2. Meanwhile, to make the ratatouille, clean the vegetables, and remove the seeds and dividing walls from the peppers. Cut the peppers, courgette and aubergine into about 1 cm (½ in) cubes. Peel and finely dice the shallot and garlic.

3. Heat the olive oil in a large saucepan, and sauté the shallot, peppers, courgette and aubergine for about 5 minutes. Add the garlic and thyme, season to taste with salt and paprika, and fry the contents of the pan for a further 2–3 minutes, until the vegetables are well browned and cooked through.

4. To serve, lift the cod fillets out of the oil, drain and arrange on plates with a little oil. Season the fish with the sea salt, black pepper and paprika, and serve with the ratatouille.

PREPARATION TIME: about 50 minutes
SERVES 4

153

MOUSSE au CHOCOLAT with SALTED CARAMEL SAUCE

FOR THE MOUSSE

150 g (5 oz) good-quality dark couverture chocolate

25 g (1 oz) butter

2 eggs (medium)

2 tsp sugar

2 tbsp Cognac (optional)

250 ml (8½ fl oz/1 cup) double (heavy) cream

FOR THE SALTED CARAMEL SAUCE

100 g (3½ oz/½ cup) sugar

200 ml (7 fl oz/scant 1 cup) cream

½ tsp sea-salt flakes

1 tbsp cocoa nibs

1. Finely chop the couverture chocolate, and slowly melt in a small saucepan together with the butter, while stirring. Remove the saucepan from the heat and allow the chocolate mixture to cool slightly. Mix one of the eggs and the yolk of the second and sugar in a round-bottomed, stainless-steel mixing bowl, and place over a hot bain-marie. Stir vigorously with a whisk until the egg foam is thick and creamy. Take the bowl off the bain-marie and continue to beat the egg foam for a short while, until lukewarm. Blend the lukewarm chocolate mixture with the egg foam, adding Cognac to taste.

2. Beat the cream until stiff, and carefully fold half at a time into the chocolate cream. Spoon the mousse into dessert rings (or small bowls), cover with cling film (plastic wrap) and refrigerate for at least 3 hours, until firm.

3. To make the sauce, slowly melt the sugar in a large saucepan over a low heat until it is golden to light brown – and to stop lumps forming, don't stir. Pour in the cream, taking great care, as it may splash. Bring the sauce to the boil, and continue to simmer over a low heat until the sugar has dissolved. Stir in the sea salt and allow the sauce to cool.

4. Lift the dessert rings from the mousse portions, then serve with the sauce and sprinkle with cocoa nibs.

PREPARATION TIME: about 50 minutes
COOLING TIME: at least 3 hours
SERVES 4-6

WHEN THE
CHEMISTRY'S RIGHT

One of the most influential couples in history met at the **SORBONNE** in Paris. The young physics and mathematics student Maria Skłodowska was at the time looking for a laboratory where she could work, so her professor introduced her to the 35-year-old Pierre Curie.

Their shared fascination with science brought the two of them closer, and in 1895 they married. The couple's unconventional behaviour is evidenced by the fact that for the wedding Marie Curie wore a lab coat, and for their honeymoon the two went on a cycling tour of France. They had two daughters, and won Nobel prizes in physics and chemistry.

In 1906 Pierre lost his life in a coach accident. Marie was hit hard by the loss, and from then on she wrote letters to him in her diary, saying how much she loved and missed him. Even though she had tragically lost Pierre, her love of science remained; as France's first female professor she took over her husband's chair at the University of Paris, and brought great success to her professorship.

GRATIN DAUPHINOIS

2 garlic cloves

300 g (10½ oz/1¼ cups) crème fraîche

200 ml (7 fl oz/scant 1 cup) milk

freshly grated nutmeg

125 g (4 oz) gruyère

1 kg (2 lb 4 oz) potatoes (preferably waxy)

butter

2 tsp thyme leaves

salt and freshly ground black pepper

1. Preheat the oven to 200°C (400°F/gas 6). Peel the garlic. Whisk the crème fraîche and milk together in a bowl, then crush the garlic and add it. Season with plenty of salt, pepper and nutmeg. Grate the cheese. Peel the potatoes and thinly slice them in a food processor.

2. Grease a gratin dish. Lay the potato slices in the dish, lightly salting now and again, and spread half the cheese over them. Pour on the crème-fraîche mixture, and top with the remaining cheese. Sprinkle with the thyme. Bake on the bottom shelf of the oven for 50–60 minutes, until the potatoes are cooked and the surface is golden brown.

PREPARATION TIME: about 30 minutes

COOKING TIME: 50–60 minutes

SERVES 4

'Life is a deep sleep of which love is the dream.'

Alfred de Musset

TARTELETTES au CITRON

FOR THE SHORTCRUST PASTRY

170 g (6 oz / 1⅓ cups) plain (all-purpose) flour

*30 g (1 oz / ⅓ cup) ground blanched **almonds** (almond meal)*

*50 g (2 oz / ¼ cup) **sugar***

pinch of salt

*125 g (4 oz) **cold butter***

*1 **egg yolk** (medium)*

FOR THE LEMON CUSTARD

*3 **eggs** (medium)*

*125 g (4 oz / ½ cup) **sugar***

*100 ml (3½ fl oz / scant ½ cup) freshly squeezed **lemon juice** (from about 5 lemons)*

*150 g (5 oz) **cold butter***

dried pulses

7 slices of lemon

icing (confectioner's) sugar

1. To make the shortcrust pastry, rub together the flour, almonds, sugar, salt and flaked butter in a bowl using your fingers, to create a fine crumb. Add the egg yolk and, if necessary, 1 tablespoon of very cold water. Rapidly knead the pastry ingredients into a smooth dough. Wrap the dough in cling film (plastic wrap) and refrigerate for 30 minutes.

2. Preheat the oven to 200°C (400°F/gas 6) and grease the tins. Roll out the pastry to a thickness of about 3 mm (⅛ in) on a lightly floured work surface, and line the tins with it. Cover the pastry with baking parchment and weigh it down with the dried pulses. Bake the tartlets for about 12 minutes, then remove the baking parchment and pulses. Bake for a further 5 minutes, until the tartlets are nicely browned and crispy. Cool, remove from the tins and allow to cool fully on a rack.

3. For the lemon custard, mix the eggs, sugar and lemon juice in a small saucepan. Slowly warm up over a low heat, stirring constantly, until the mixture has a thick custardy consistency (this will take about 10 minutes). If you have a kitchen thermometer, at 80°C (175°F) the lemon custard will be ready. Immediately remove the saucepan from the heat, and pass the custard through a fine-meshed sieve and into a bowl. Cool for a few minutes until lukewarm. Finely dice the cold butter, and mix with the luke-warm lemon custard using a hand-held blender. Spoon the custard into the tartlets, cover, and refrigerate for 2 hours.

4. To serve, arrange the lemon slices on the filling and dust the tartelets with icing sugar.

PREPARATION TIME: about 1 hour · **COOLING TIME:** 30 minutes
BAKING TIME: about 17 minutes · **COOLING TIME:** at least 2 hours
MAKES 7

CURLY ENDIVE
with POACHED EGG, BACON and WALNUTS

½ *curly endive*

1–2 *garlic cloves*

3 tbsp *sherry vinegar*

1 heaped tsp **Dijon mustard**

1 tsp **mild honey**

3 tbsp **walnut oil**

3 tbsp **olive oil**

75 g (2½ oz) **smoked streaky bacon**

60 g (2 oz) **walnuts**

4 very fresh **eggs** *(medium)*

2 tbsp **white wine vinegar**

salt and freshly ground **black pepper**

1 baguette or *farmhouse bread*

1. Clean and wash the curly endive, then dry in a salad spinner. To make the vinaigrette, peel and very finely chop the garlic. Mix with the sherry vinegar, mustard, honey, garlic, a generous pinch of salt and plenty of pepper. Drizzle in both oils to create a creamy sauce.

2. Cut the bacon into thin strips and coarsely chop the nuts. Briefly render the bacon in a hot pan with no added fat until crispy, then remove and briefly toast the nuts in the remaining bacon fat.

3. For the poached eggs, bring 500 ml (17 fl oz/2 cups) of water and the white wine vinegar to the boil in a small saucepan. Break each egg into a cup. Remove the saucepan from the heat, bringing the water off the boil. Stir the water with a wooden spoon to form a slight vortex. Slowly slide the eggs into the vortex one after another. Wrap the whites around the yolks with a wooden spoon. Poach the eggs in the water for 3–4 minutes. Remove with a slotted spoon and drain on paper towel.

4. Pull the curly endive into small pieces, mix with the vinaigrette and serve with the nuts, bacon and poached egg. Serve with slices of baguette or farmhouse bread.

PREPARATION TIME: about 30 minutes
SERVES 4

165

FAVOURITE RECIPES
WITH A HEART

168

SPRING
FEVER

Vichyssoise
113

Moules Marinières
40

Coq au Vin Blanc
70

Crème Brûlée
33

SWEET
TEMPTATION

Tarte Tatin
43

Madeleines
98

Paris-Brest
15

Chocolate Macarons
57

TEMPESTUOUS
PASSION

Melon Salad
with Ham and Basil
120

Mini Croques-madame
150

Canelés de Bordeaux
140

ON CLOUD
NINE

Tuna Rillette
81

Parisian Onion Soup
125

Artichokes
with Sauce Gribiche
37

Salade Niçoise
16

Oysters au Gratin
with Mornay Sauce
102

Côte de Bœuf
with Sauce Béarnaise
29

Cheese Soufflé
36

Mousse au Chocolat
with Salted Caramel Sauce
154

169

INDEX

171

172

SOURCES

Abelard, Peter and Radice, Betty *The Letters of Abelard and Héloïse*. Re-edition, Penguin Classics, 1974.

Baudelaire, Charles, *The Flowers of Evil*. New Directions, 1946.

Hugo, Victor, *Les Misérables*. Translated by Charles E. Wilbour. Carleton Publishing Company, 1862.

Hugo, Victor, *The Hunchback of Notre-Dame*. Translated by Frederic Shoberl. Richard Bentley, 1833.

TEAM

ANNE-KATRIN WEBER — *Recipe development, food & styling*

Anne-Katrin Weber, from Hamburg, is a chef, nutritionist and food stylist, and the author of numerous cookery and baking books. As far back as she can remember she has found France inspirational and has traversed her favourite country as much as possible, sometimes seeking out the sun in the south and sometimes the wind in the north, but always in quest of buttery croissants, aromatic cheeses and fine wines.

WWW.ANNEKATRINWEBER.DE | WWW.VEGGIELICIOUS.DE

JULIA HOERSCH — *Recipe photography*

Julia Hoersch has for many years worked in Hamburg as a freelance photographer and is passionate about her photography work for countless prestigious magazines, agencies and publishers.

With *In Love with Paris* she has been able to realise a project that is truly close to her heart.

WWW.JULIAHOERSCH.DE

NATHALIE GEFFROY — *Paris photography*

Nathalie Geffroy is a graphic designer and photographer. She loves roaming the streets of Paris with her camera, savouring the city's numerous features and capturing a host of unique moments on film for posterity.

WWW.NATHPARIS.NET

MIRIAM STROBACH — *Graphic design*

Born in Bavaria, lives in Vienna, studied information design in Graz and discovered her love of things culinary in Paris. As a co-founder of Le Foodink she conceives and designs projects in the field of food and drink.

WWW.LEFOODINK.COM

This edition published in 2021 by Hardie Grant Books, an imprint of Hardie Grant Publishing
First published in 2021 by Hölker Verlag in der Coppenrath Verlag GmbH & Co. KG, Hafenweg 30, 48155
Münster, Germany. Original title: Verliebt in Paris. Rezepte und Geschichten (ISBN 978-3-88117-239-4)
All rights reserved.

Hardie Grant Books (London)
5th & 6th Floors
52–54 Southwark Street
London SE1 1UN

Hardie Grant Books (Melbourne)
Building 1, 658 Church Street
Richmond, Victoria 3121

hardiegrantbooks.com

British Library Cataloguing-in-Publication Data. A catalogue record for this book is available from the
British Library.

In Love with Paris
ISBN: 9781784884727

10 9 8 7 6

176

IDEA AND CONCEPT: Hölker Verlag
MOOD AND RECIPE PHOTOGRAPHY: Nathalie Geffroy and Julia Hoersch
RECIPE DEVELOPMENT, FOOD AND STYLING: Anne-Katrin Weber
ILLUSTRATIONS: Nicole Tilinski
LAYOUT AND TYPESETTING: Miriam Strobach
EDITORS: Franziska Grünewald und Muriel Magon
PRODUCTION: Anja Bergmann
LITHOGRAPHY: FSM Premedia GmbH & Co. KG, Münster

PUBLISHER: Kajal Mistry
TYPESETTING: David Meikle
TRANSLATION: William Sleath
PROOFREADERS: Caroline West and Sarah Herman
INDEXER: Cathy Heath
PRODUCTION CONTROLLER: Nikolaus Ginelli

Colour reproduction by p2d
Printed and bound in China by Leo Paper Products Ltd.